CHASING CARSON

CHASING CARSON

A FAMILY'S JOURNEY THROUGH ADOLESCENCE, ADDICTION AND RECOVERY

Dawn McCord

www.AdolescentAddictionandRecovery.com

Columbus, Ohio

Chasing Carson: A Family's Journey through Adolescence, Addiction, and Recovery

Published by Gatekeeper Press
2167 Stringtown Rd., Suite 109
Columbus, OH 43123-2989
www.GatekeeperPress.com

Library of Congress Control Number: 2021947004

ISBN (paperback): 9781662919862
eISBN: 9781662919879

To both my bubba wubbas

For you I'll risk it all

Introduction

Today's the day . . . it's raining out and we are all under a "shelter in place" order in our state of Indiana during the COVID-19 pandemic of 2020. I am a hairdresser who usually works from home, and due to not being able to practice social distancing, I am out of a job for a while. My college-age son, Jackson, sits next to me with his earbuds in watching his professor's lecture on WebEx.

It is a different world right now, filled with a lot of uncertainty. Are we taking this virus seriously or are we overreacting? I personally would err on the side of caution. I closed my business and canceled my clients a week before it was mandated.

Clients, friends, and family have asked . . . "Are you scared?"

I said, "No, after nearly losing a child . . . no other crisis compares."

I don't mean to trivialize the seriousness of this illness and how it will affect the health and financial aspects of people's lives. It might be all relative, but from a mother's perspective, losing a child or watching them nearly die . . . well, nothing else matters.

This is our story.

- In the State of Indiana, approximately 90 percent of individuals with addiction begin using illicit drugs before the age of eighteen. Since 1999, the number of opioid poisoning deaths increased by 500%. (MPH, In.gov)

- Analysis from the Substance Abuse and Mental Health Services Administration states that as addicts need stronger painkillers to achieve the same effect, they may be unable to access pills through their healthcare provider or unable to afford illegally sold pills. Some end up switching to heroin, a cheaper illegal opioid. (www.usafacts.org, published May 20, 2019, SAMHSA.gov data review 2013)

- Addiction is one of the most common mental illnesses in the United States, affecting millions of Americans every day. An estimated 21 million Americans ages twelve or older (7.8 percent of the population) required treatment for substance abuse in 2016, according to the Substance Abuse and Mental Health Administration. (Alvernia University, Oct. 25, 2017)

- Although the addiction process is similar for adults and adolescents, it happens more quickly for teenagers. If substance abuse begins in adulthood, it can take eight to ten years for an individual to reach chronic stages of dependency. If the onset is during adolescence, it can take less than fifteen months. (Dick Schaefer, *Choices and Consequences*)

1.

...and Mary wept

October 18, 2019

"Carson, wake up and go to bed . . . Carson . . . Carson . . . "

Sloan turns the light on in the living room and screams "Carson!"

It's 4:30 in the morning and Sloan, my husband, has just gone downstairs to start his day when I hear him scream. I jump out of bed and run down the stairs to find Sloan trying to revive our son.

Carson is gray and gasping for breath. He has vomited on his shoulder. I scream and run back upstairs for the Narcan that I bought one and a half years ago . . . "just in case." I grab my phone and call 911. I scream into the phone, "My son is overdosing, please help!"

I am fumbling with the Narcan vial, trying to read the directions (this is an old type of dose, intramuscular), as I'm trying to tell the dispatcher what I'm trying to do, and she is attempting to guide me.

I drop the dose, then pick it up. I know I only have moments to get this into him. I have no idea how long he has been like this . . . has he aspirated? I get the two parts together and try to shoot it into his thigh, but I had it put together wrong and the Narcan liquid just runs down his leg! I am losing my son. I run to the front door to open it for the paramedics . . . the door is old, the lock sticks. I can't fucking open the door. Finally, it opens and the paramedics come in and take over-- there are three!

More firemen arrive. When the police arrive there are two officers, but all I hear is, "Ma'am, what did your son take?"

"I don't know! He has a history of substance abuse; he was just in treatment all summer!"

I hear, "He's going to pass out, Sir . . . Sir, sit down . . . Ma'am, get your husband some water."

I run to the kitchen to get water, the whole time screaming, "Oh my God, no, please no!"

The paramedics have given Carson a dose of Narcan through his nose, they have started an IV of Narcan, and they have bagged him to help him breathe. He hasn't come to yet.

Isn't he supposed to come to after Narcan?!

The police officer asks, "Is this his wallet on the table?"

"Yes," I say.

"Can you please look through it and show me the contents?" he asks.

I open the wallet to find a straw and a baggy of powder. The police officer with gloves on takes it from me and says, "It looks like heroin."

"Heroin?! Heroin?! What?! Nooooo!"

"Ma'am, you need to go wash your hands. We don't know if it's laced with fentanyl."

Wait, what?! How'd we get here? How did experimenting with pot end up with my son overdosing on heroin?!

I notice that in the frenzy of everyone doing something to help Carson, there is an older man, a fireman, leaning up against the wall just watching with an expression of judgment. I can't believe I am noticing this. Like, what the hell? Has he seen so much that he is just disgusted? I have the wherewithal, or call it God, but I take pictures of the whole ordeal. If Carson makes it through, he has to see what he is doing to himself . . . to us. They wheel him out and ask what hospital. I say, "Community North."

Before Sloan and I go upstairs to put clothes on, I call my dad, screaming and crying, telling my eighty-one-year-old father that my son just overdosed, and that I'm not sure if he's going to make it. I hang up with him and I call my childhood best friend. She answers on the first ring. It's almost 5:00 a.m. now.

"What's wrong?!" she says.

I say, "He overdosed, Mern. Carson overdosed on heroin!"

"Is he alive?" she asks tentatively.

"As of when they took him out the door he was, but he hadn't come to. We are heading to Community North, I'll let you know . . . "

It's roughly 5:20 a.m. when we arrive at the hospital. The ER desk says he has arrived and that they'll let us know when we can go back and see him. He's alive! I turn around to see Suzie and Shane, my best friends since I was twelve years old, standing in front of Sloan and me. We collapse in their arms.

What seems like hours is still just minutes until they call us back to see him. He is sedated because he finally came to in the ambulance and was agitated. They have him all wired up, IV in his arm, and he is tied to his bed. Nurses and doctors come in and introduce themselves. They order tests, saying they need to stabilize him. I text our church friends to tell them what is going on and ask for prayers. This isn't the first time Sloan and I have called on them to pray for Carson.

Julie, an oncology nurse and church friend, shows up. She walked across the hospital campus immediately after getting the text. She starts to explain everything going on.

Carson starts to become conscious. It's obvious he's still high. He says he's "Got to pee." He tries to get out of bed before realizing his arms are attached to the bed. "What the fuck?" he says.

I try to reason with him, and he says he can't hear me, so I speak louder, Julie speaks louder, the other female nurse speaks louder.

Nothing, he can't hear us.

We finally write it down on paper. Doctors and lab people come in and out doing tests, his oxygen saturation rate keeps dipping, and they put an oxygen mask on him, which he keeps trying to take off. His blood pressure hovers dangerously low. They start administering antibiotics through the IV because they fear he has pneumonia due to aspirating his vomit. They decide to move him to ICU . . .

Did Mary, Mother of God, weep? Absolutely!

2.

poly-substance use is higher among adolescents

~ Dick Schaefer, *Choices and Consequences*

It's August 2017, two years before the overdose, and Carson has just finished his first week of his sophomore year of high school and a week's worth of football practice. The state fair is in full swing. We had a lovely summer. Carson's older brother, Jackson, went on a church mission trip to Haiti, and Carson and I went to visit our family friend's house in England and on to France for two weeks.

In those countries, as most know, the culture is quite liberal about letting teenagers drink. Even though I do not drink, Sloan and I agreed to let Carson drink on this trip. I struggled with that since both mine and my husband's fathers were alcoholics, but I hoped that maybe Carson could learn how to drink responsibly.

On Sunday of that week, we decide to meet grandma and grandpa (my parents) for lunch so the boys could tell them about their trips and show pictures. We wake the boys to get showers and get moving. I'm in the shower when Carson comes in and asks when I'll be out.

"Why?" I ask him.

"Because, I have to take a shower."

"Carson, you just took a shower."

"Oh, yeah . . . I'm half-asleep."

Strange, I think.

We get to the restaurant and Carson is walking across the parking lot like he's drunk. I say to him, "What is up with you?" We sit down with the grandparents and order our food. Jackson tells them about his trip, but I'm watching Carson and notice he is having trouble keeping his eyes open and his movements have slowed. I look toward Sloan, who is also watching him. Suddenly, in the middle of conversation, Carson scoots his chair back from the table and yells, "I gotta take a piss."

"Carson, keep your voice down!" I say between gritted teeth. "You know where the bathroom is, go!"

I look at Jackson and say, "Go with him."

Jackson comes back to the table and says, "He's fine."

No! He is not fine! Something is terribly wrong. During all this, Sloan and I are trying to distract the grandparents, so they won't notice. It's not working. The final straw is when I jump up to say we have to go, and Carson, now back at the table, drools and spits on the floor.

I apologize to my parents as we quickly exit the restaurant. I am screaming in my head . . . what is going on?!

As we get in the car, I start to interrogate Carson. "What is going on with you? Are you on something?"

He starts to get defensive and lies through his teeth. It's obvious that he has taken something.

"Carson, tell me what you took. You are not right; we need to get you to the hospital to find out what it is."

As Sloan pulls up to the house, Carson jumps out of the car. He flips us off as he starts to leave. Sloan is yelling, "You can't leave, get back to the house."

Nothing . . . no response.

Carson keeps on walking toward our village.

"Jackson, what do you know?!"

"I don't know, Mom, I swear. I'll get on Snapchat and find out."

I call Carson's friend's mom to see what she knows. She had driven a bunch of the guys to the state fair the day before. I tell her what happened at lunch and that he has just left. She tells me she'll ask her son and get back to me. I text my church chicks and tell them what is going on. We, as couples, were to go to dinner. Their husbands start calling

Sloan, asking if they should come over and help. Sloan tells them to hang tight. Carson's friend's mom calls me back and says her son was in tears and told her that several of the guys decided to pool their money, and Carson was going to sneak out and buy Xan bars, a street form of Xanax that is more potent and can be laced with other chemicals. Her son says Carson took one or two last night.

"Oh, my God! What if this fries his brain?"

I am walking up and down the street in front of our house and responding to texts from church friends asking if he has come back, all while trying to call and text Carson to come home. He doesn't answer.

About two hours later, he comes home. He is agitated and says we just need to leave him alone, that it'll be OK. I plead with him to go to the hospital to make sure that whatever he took was not laced with anything. He screams, "No!" and says he doesn't want to live at home anymore, and that we just need to get off his case. He tries to leave again, and I call 911. The police arrive and Carson seems to be able to keep his shit together to answer their questions. They say he needs to go to the hospital, and he's either going with us or them. He chooses us and we jump in the car and take off.

Sloan is driving, and I am talking with Carson as calmly as I can. He is so emotional when he speaks, saying we don't understand, and that it is so hard being a teenager. I carefully turn on the video on my phone to document how he is acting. He realizes what I am doing, and he goes ballistic. He starts to try to kick his way out of the backseat window. He is kicking and flailing so hard, the car is shaking from side to side going up the highway. I call 911, telling them what is happening, and they patch me through to the security at the hospital.

I tell them that I know he'll bolt when we pull up. He is sixteen years old and Lord only knows what he is on. We get there and three police officers walk out to the car and escort him into the hospital. Again, he seems to calm his shit down in front of the police and the nurses. They get us into a room, take his blood, and start an IV. Carson is visibly agitated, and he starts to "pick" on Sloan.

"Why are you here? You don't fucking need to be here. You can stay, Mom, but he needs to fucking leave."

Sloan leaves and goes to the waiting room. The nurse and doctor come in and out asking questions, getting labs. Carson starts to fall asleep. Oh, thank God, please, Lord, let him sleep it off.

A nurse asks me to step out of the room. She pats my arm and says, "You are not alone, we see this a lot lately."

What? This? *This* is not the norm for our family. *This* does not happen in our family. He is an honor roll student, a tight end on the high school football team, a talented baseball catcher who gets player of the week during the season. "This" is not Carson!

I walk back into the room, and he jolts awake and again is so agitated that he says, "What were you fucking saying? Were you talking about me? This is bullshit, Mom! You better get me out of here, or I am walking out."

At that moment he rips the IV out of his arm and is gushing blood everywhere. I run out of the room screaming, "He is going to leave . . . he's bleeding . . . he ripped his IV out . . . help!!!"

The nurses come in, along with one of the police officers who escorted him in. They get him settled. The police officer says, "You need to calm down, son, or I'm going to walk you over to behavioral health and they will keep you up to seventy-two hours."

I think to myself, *please take him so he can come down!* As we are waiting for the results of the blood tests, Carson looks at me with such distain. I try to remain calm and not talk. I don't want to set him off again.

He says, "You know, this is just a waste of time, and you are wasting money." I say nothing. I keep searching on my phone for how to get him into our local recovery hospital. They stop taking assessments at 8:00 p.m., and it's nearly 8:00 p.m. now . . . we are not going to make it.

Carson gets up and starts pacing the room, then goes out in the hallway and walks up to the double doors. I look at the nurses sitting at the main desk as they just watch him. He pushes the doors open and starts to leave. I say,

"Do something!" This stops him and he comes back into the room, looking at me like he's disgusted.

The police officer comes back and says to Carson, "Well, son, it looks like we will be taking a walk after you are released from here."

The nurse comes in with the results. Carson has tested positive for THC, Benzodiazepine, and some other unidentifiable chemical.

Sloan joins us as the police officer leads us through back halls of the hospital to the behavioral health area. Carson is still fixated on Sloan being the bad guy and steers clear of him and lags behind. I'm concerned he is going to run, but the officer just plods ahead . . . he seems unconcerned. We get to the intake area of the behavioral health wing. All doors are locked and there are cameras in all corners. The police officer buzzes the intercom and explains that Carson needs an eval. Someone comes to get him, and we are not allowed to go back with him.

About an hour goes by, and a guy in scrubs comes out with Carson and says they don't see any reason to keep him. Really?! They say he is probably coming down and will be fine soon. OK?!

We head home.

3.

Levels of use are harder to determine in adolescents

~ Dick Schaefer, *Choices and Consequences*

As we walk through the door, Jackson is waiting for us. Carson blows past him and runs up the stairs to his room. Jackson says, "Mom, he has more."

"What? How do you know?"

"It seems that Carson and his friends had forty or sixty dollars, and that was supposed to buy eight Xans."

"We need to check his wallet," I say to Sloan now.

I run upstairs as Jackson gets into the shower. Carson is lying on his bed facedown. "Carson, where is your wallet?"

"I don't know."

I start to pull at his covers to put them over him, thinking he will fall asleep. I see his wallet sticking out from underneath his leg. I grab it and start to look through it.

"Stop, Mom, stop, that's not fucking yours."

"Carson, do you have any more pills? Where did you put them?" There is nothing in his wallet.

Carson blows up and says, "I'm done with you all!"

He starts to go down the hall and in a fit of rage pulls an 11 by 16 collage frame off the wall. I am begging him to stay. I scream over the banister, "He's going to leave!" It's nearly midnight at this point. Sloan comes barreling around the corner and tackles Carson on the stairs. I am screaming, "Should I call 911, should I call the police?"

Sloan is holding on tight as Carson beats on Sloan's back and tries to wiggle out of his grasp. I scream for Jackson and he hears me from the shower. Jackson comes running out of the bathroom soaking wet with a towel around his waist. He climbs over Sloan to get to Carson and tries to tell Carson we just want to help him.

Carson seems to have superhuman strength, because he gets away from Jackson and Sloan. All three end up in the kitchen slammed against the counter where a vase falls and shatters on the granite countertop. I've called 911 and the police are on their way. Carson gets away from them again and ends up in the living room where he is trying to climb out the window. Sloan grabs him with a bear-hug grip from behind and pulls him out of the window. Carson rears back and headbutts Sloan to where they flip over the back of the couch.

Jack is screaming, "I have got to knock him out."

Jackson knocks Carson hard enough to stun him, and he lands on the floor in front of the TV. He is exhausted and starts crying. "I need to just sleep," he says.

Jackson gets him up and Carson says he wants to sleep with Jackson. It's crazy because Jackson just punched him. Despite the two year age difference and Carson's need to compete with Jackson, they have a strong brotherly bond.

As they make their way to Jackson's bedroom, I start thinking about the erratic thoughts and emotions, the violence, all from being on this drug. At this point, Carson has been under the influence for twenty-four hours. We don't know how many he has taken, but we cannot find any pills. The police come, and we explain what just ensued. They take a look around, and they talk to Carson, who is now lying in the fetal position on Jackson's bed. They inform us that there is really nothing they can do, he seems to be calming down, and he'll be fine.

What?! The hell we are living just keeps going on!

4.

Your finest moment may well be your darkest. And you will be a parent.

~ Michael J. Bradley, Ed.D., *Yes, Your Teen is Crazy!*

As Sunday turns into Monday, Carson rambles around the house throughout the night. If he slept, it was very little. In fact, I don't think he has eaten since that one chicken tender at lunch on Sunday. He hasn't even had anything to drink. Sloan and I wake up, and we pray that when Carson wakes, he will be back to normal. I call school and tell them he is sick. Sloan calls work and explains that he is trying to get his son into rehab. I call my clients and say I need to reschedule them. When I get to our pastor, Jamalyn, who was to be my noon appointment, I tell her the truth. I call the recovery hospital and tell them what has transpired over the past twenty-four hours. The soonest time they have for an assessment is 10:00 a.m. Tuesday. I'm devastated and hope we can hold on.

We hear stirring upstairs; he's awake. The shower turns on and we are holding our breath. Moments later, with his hair sopping wet, he comes through the porch where we are sitting. His gait is off. He is slightly stooped, and he has this hooded look. He is not normal. Oh my God!

"Carson, we have an appointment at Fairbanks Recovery Hospital tomorrow morning."

"Why?" he says.

"Because, it's obvious there is a problem and you clearly are not sober."

This sets him off again. He grabs his backpack and leaves. Jackson wakes up and asks where Carson is. We tell him that Carson is still high, and we have no idea how it can last that long.

Jackson says, "Mom, Dad, I think he took all the pills. From what everyone is saying on Snapchat, he has been trying to get more or buy some weed."

I'm freaking out! "Jackson, see if you can find him." It's close to noon and Josh, our youth director calls.

"Hey, how ya'll doing? Jamalyn told me what's going on with Carson."

I tell Josh what has happened over the past day and that Carson got up and was still not right and left about 10:30 a.m. Josh says he'll come home for lunch and look for him—he and his wife live a block away. Josh texts and says he's found him.

Carson, at first, does not recognize Josh. This is hard to do because Josh is 6'5" with a full beard-- a big, impressive guy. Carson is with some other guys and he describes them to me. No one I know.

He says, "It seems he has smoked some pot and is looking for more. I gave him some food and water. I think he just needs to come down, these guys seem to be watching over him. I'm heading back to church, I'll check-in in a bit."

A couple hours later a girlfriend persuades Carson to come home, and she brings him. Immediately after she leaves, he is agitated and again looks at Sloan like he's the devil. Jackson tries to talk to him and tell him all his friends are worried about him and that they wondered why he wasn't at school.

Carson has forgotten that it's not still summer break, and he started school a week ago. Carson heads up to his room and within minutes, he's back down saying that he can't live in this house anymore, and that I need to divorce Sloan. He is so irrational . . . has he taken more Xans? He says he's going to go stay at a friend's house, a friend we do not know.

I am talking calmly and agreeing with him just to make sure he doesn't bolt again. We just need to get to Tuesday at 10:00 a.m. to the assessment. Jackson takes over to keep him engaged and at home. I just wish he would pass out! He has barely slept, eaten or drank anything in thirty-six hours.

During this time, Sloan and I are calling school, the football coach, parents of his good friends. We respond to church friends who are checking in. We are completely at a loss! As Sloan is talking on the phone, he is walking around in the backyard and he hears something fall from Carson's upstairs window. It's a backpack, and Carson is trying to climb out.

Sloan goes running through the house, and up the stairs to stop him. Because Carson is so hyperfocused on Sloan being the bad guy, this does not end well. Again, I call 911 for help.

Officer O'Conner arrives. He's been the neighborhood patrolman for years. He has watched the kids in the neighborhood grow up. He grew up in this area and went to the local Catholic high school. He has yet to be called to the house during this ordeal. Sloan and I meet him outside and explain what we are going through.

He shakes his head and tells us, "Can't they just smoke some weed and call it a day?" He seems frustrated with all of "it." He tells us he keeps eyes on the teens that congregate in our village. At the McDonald's, the art center, down by the river . . . he says drug dealers approach these kids and offer up their latest "goodies" and or offer them to peddle their "goods."

We live in an area of Indianapolis considered Midtown. We have several Catholic, private, and public schools within a five-mile radius. Families choose to live here because of the diversity. Our village hosts many art galleries and restaurants, which bring people from the surrounding areas to visit.

Sloan and I are truly not surprised. We grew up in this area, we too have been the teens that push the envelope, but why does it feel so different? Is it the opiate crisis that our country has been fighting? Is it the accessibility, due to social media? Is it because now, it's our kids?

Officer O'Conner goes into the house to speak to Carson. A few minutes later, he comes out with Carson. Carson sits on the steps. Officer O'Conner has called for the EMTs to come check him out. He is trying to find a way to get Carson into Fairbanks sooner than tomorrow morning. Carson keeps his act together.

The EMT is a man in his sixties who checks Carson out. He is stable. I scream in my head "No! He is not!" Josh pulls up to check in before going home. He is startled by the ambulance and officer.

Carson asked if he could go back into the house. We all say yes.

Josh asks, "What's up?" We say we are trying to find a way to get Carson to Fairbanks sooner than tomorrow at 10:00 a.m.

The EMT replies with, "His stats are normal, so really I can't take him."

Officer O'Conner says, "With the way the laws are, if I take him, he'll go through the ER again, but not on to Fairbanks."

We are at a loss.

Finally, Josh says, "Well, I'll keep him distracted for as long as I can and then bring him home to hopefully crash." Thank you, Jesus! Josh goes inside to get Carson and they head off to a restaurant.

Around 11:00 p.m., Josh brings Carson home. I think, "Oh, he'll be back to his old self."

Nope . . .

His gait is still off and he has that hooded look. Carson heads upstairs. Josh tells us they talked about everything and Carson ate very little, but that Josh was able to convince Carson to go with us to be "checked out" at Fairbanks the next morning.

5.

"A period of forced abstinence during the formative teenage years is better than that same time spent on drugs."

~ David Sheff, *Beautiful Boy*

It's Tuesday morning. It has probably been sixty hours since Carson has taken his first Xan bar. In that time, we know that he has taken anywhere from six to eight bars. He has smoked pot, eaten very little, drank even less and slept maybe a couple hours each night since Saturday. I have called 911 five times. There's been one trip to the ER, one visit to the behavioral health portion of the hospital and a "check-up" from a paramedic. Carson is awake and in the shower, but he is still under some sort of influence. He might not be feeling the euphoria of the Xanax, but the leftover effects are lingering. It's a type of hangover.

I'm nervous. Is he going to say he won't go to Fairbanks? Will he bolt, again?

Sloan and I are ready to go, and Carson walks right past us, out the door and says, "Let's get this over with."

We enter through the assessment wing of Fairbanks and have to buzz into the receptionist. They tell us someone will be with us shortly. Carson sits down. His leg is bouncing up and down a mile a minute. Sloan and I keep our mouths shut in fear he'll walk right out the door. An intake counselor greets us and leads us back to a private room. She is quite friendly and asks Carson if he is hungry or thirsty. She tells us we can keep our phones, but my purse will have to be locked up in the cabinet. She starts to ask us questions about demographics and insurance.

Carson's knee is still just bouncing like crazy and he can't stop looking at his phone. I'm not sure if he is Snapchatting or texting or what. The counselor says she'll be right back.

Carson turns to Sloan and me, who are sitting behind him, because Sloan is trying to not agitate him, with this sideways look of disgust and says, "You know this is a fucking waste of time?"

The counselor comes back in and asks us to step out so she can talk to Carson alone.

About thirty minutes later, she comes out and takes Sloan and me across the hall to ask us questions. This allows us time to tell our version of events leading to why we are here. I show her the videos I have taken over the past forty-eight hours. I tell her he is still not right. I can tell he is wound tight. We can't keep him at home, we are afraid he'll leave and try to find more of something to get high. We finish and go back in with Carson.

She tells us all that they have to wait for authorization from our insurance before they tell us what his care plan might be. We've been here an hour and a half, and then another hour leads to another until finally insurance gives an authorization.

During this time of waiting, Carson is like a caged animal and several times he has jumped up and walked to the locked doors as though he is going to leave. We plead with him. I call Josh and say, "He's going to bolt, what do we do?" Other counselors come out of their offices and talk calmly with Carson. They walk up and down the hall with him. They calm him down for the time being.

I say to one of them, "What happens if he leaves?"

They say, "Since he is a minor, are you willing to call him in as a runaway?"

Wow . . . at this point, we say yes, because it's the safest thing for him.

It's around 6:00 p.m. Tuesday, and we have been at Fairbanks assessing and waiting since 10:00 a.m. The process is long but most of the wait is waiting for insurance to authorize some sort of care. At this point, we'll mortgage the house because we need help!

Finally, someone from the adolescent unit comes to get him, and we follow. When we get to the wing where he'll be staying, we meet a few of the other kids that are on the unit and then the staff member says it's time to say our goodbyes. I start to tear up as Carson turns to hug me. He laughs and says, "It'll be OK, Mom."

Sloan and I walk out the front door of Fairbanks, and I collapse on the sidewalk. The sob that comes out of me Sloan hasn't heard since I said goodbye to my mom as she passed away. It is guttural. It is breath-sucking. The heartbreak I felt from leaving my child (albeit sixteen years old) in a locked wing for substance abuse is debilitating.

Sloan finally gets me up and into the car. It's time to tell the family what has transpired over the last three days. As we drive home to get clothes for Carson, I make the calls. I can't get the words out without sobbing. My cousin Eric, who is more like my brother, can't understand me. Sloan has to take the phone and explain. I don't know how he's doing it. I think he is in shock from all that we've been through so far.

Unfortunately, this is just the first of many years of us chasing Carson.

6.

Keep 'em alive to twenty-five.

~ Frances E. Jensen, MD, *The Teenage Brain*

In the book *Beautiful Boy*, David Sheff says that he wished he could have forced Nic, his son, into a long-term rehabilitation program when Nic was still a minor. David Sheff writes that forcing anyone into rehab before they are ready and able to understand the principles of recovery may not prevent relapse. However, he feels any period of forced abstinence during the formative teenage years is better than the same time spent on drugs.

Carson spent nine days in inpatient, where he detoxed, and then nine days in partial hospitalization where he slept at home, but then spent twelve hours a day at Fairbanks. His program then progressed down to intensive outpatient. He went to Fairbanks three hours a night, three nights a week for eight weeks. He missed three weeks of school at the beginning of his sophomore year, but was able to do classwork at Fairbanks thanks to the wonderful counselors at his high school.

During these weeks of rehab, we as a family would attend weekly group sessions with other families and their teens in the program. We attended parent-only education classes, learning all about adolescence and addiction. So many parents or caregivers looked like deer in headlights. The anguish can be suffocating.

Carson did not participate much during his outpatient programming, and he held fast that he was not an addict. He still was defensive about why he was going through all this. He claimed that he was a teenager and this was what teenagers do. He never claimed he would stop smoking pot. In fact, none of the kids in group thought pot was that big of deal. This age-old battle is still a battle with the youth.

Carson's last outpatient day, on which he "graduated" from the program, was the start of fall break. We let him have his best buds spend the night. We thought it would be a reward for sticking with the program. I woke up later that night to go to the restroom, and as I checked on the boys, I noticed Carson was missing.

"Where's Carson?"

They all say he's in the bathroom. I walk in, and Carson is puking his guts up.

I said, "What the hell, Carson?"

He says he's got a serious headache.

"What did you take?" I go upstairs to his room and rummage around. I find a crushed can of Four Loko. This drink has 12-14% alcohol and a crapload of caffeine in twenty-four ounces.

I don't get it. What is going on?

7.

*130 people die from opioid overdoses
every day in the USA.*

CDC.gov

We made it through the rest of Carson's sophomore year relatively unscathed, meaning we noticed no other signs of drug use. There were times we knew he was "up to something" or we smelled the horrific smell of pot smoke after going to bed. I found bottles of empty beer stuck in peculiar places in the house. But I could never tell who took them, Jackson or Carson.

I am an active reader; I have read everything on "raising" boys. Everything from *What to Expect When You're Expecting* to *Yes, Your Teen is Crazy: Loving Your Kid without Losing Your Mind.* I have read books on educating boys, on disciplining boys, on the emotional stability of boys. I have learned that in an effort to understand them, I could not prevent their choices, whether good or bad. And in adolescence, the choices seem to be more bad than good.

Sloan and I started to waver in our stance toward substance use. We thought if we said to the boys, "Just stick with pot," they would actually stick with pot. I thought that if I let Carson and Jackson drink "on special occasions," like vacations, that the temptation to "experiment" further would be less enticing. My dad, an abstinent alcoholic, always advised against this, saying it's not legal, not that it could lead to early abuse. I thought that other cultures let their twelve-year-olds drink wine or beer and those countries don't have as much drug and alcohol abuse.

Or do they?

As sophomore year moved into summer break, and summer break into Carson's junior year, we started to "catch" Carson acting "just not right." We found ourselves threatening drug tests and having knock-down-drag-outs with him. He was either defensive and stuck to his innocence or he was so compliant that later I found out he was manipulating us. He went to school. He was getting good grades. Though there were a couple times we suspected that he might be cheating. He got suspended for having a vape on campus. All the while, he claimed innocence or blamed someone or something else. One of the lessons we learned in parent-only education at Fairbanks was that it is really hard to tell if the manipulative signs of substance abuse are what they are. The signs and symptoms of substance abuse and adolescence are the same or similar. You find yourself thinking you're crazy. You second-guess yourself. You worry. It's maddening.

Labor Day weekend of Carson's junior year, he and some friends go to another friend's lake house. We are friends with the parents. All is cool, they are planning a fun weekend. About 10:00 p.m. the first night they all are there, I get a call from DNR in Parke County.

"Ma'am, is your son Carson?"

"Yes?" I say, my pitch going up as if I'm not sure. I'm too nervous for my heart to even race as I wait to hear what the person on the other end of the phone will say.

"Ma'am, I have caught your son and his friends on state park property after hours and they have marijuana and paraphernalia in their possession. You need to come get him."

I tell him I am an hour away and he is staying with one of the boys who is in his custody. I am in the middle of texting his dad to say that the boys are in trouble. He responds, "Yes, I am just getting the voicemail now. Service is spotty here." He says he'll sort it out.

Carson walks through the door early the next day, and we are shocked but not surprised. He is remorseful. He says we might get something in the mail from Marion County in regard to the citation in Parke County. He goes to his room, where he spends 95% of his time. I find myself in his room, talking to his back as he faces the computer.

"Carson, I think it's time to talk to someone, an addiction therapist."

Carson tells me, "Not now, Mom."

I continue, "Carson, I can't tell what is going on with you, but as your mother, I know something is up. I think you need to get a handle on your substance use."

He starts to cry and screams at me to leave his room. I press on, because, well, it's what I do, and I don't know what else to do. I want him to say "*Yes, Mom. I have a problem and I want to see someone.*" But I know that it's not going to happen.

He finally says "Fine! Go ahead and set up the appointment."

Jackson is home from college for the holiday weekend. He has been hanging out with his friend Joey all day in the village. I text him that family dinner is at 6:30 p.m.

He says, "Can I have another half hour?"

"No," I say, "get home."

He walks into the backyard and sits at the table. He says he's not hungry but will sit at the table while we eat and visit. He stands up to go in through the porch to get a drink and projectile vomits all over.

"What the fuck, Jackson? What is going on?!"

I lose my shit! I am so done. "Carson gets busted with pot and now you? What did you take?"

"Nothing," he says.

"Bullshit!" I yell back, furious and scared.

As I am cursing at him, Sloan is trying to clean up the vomit. I'm the yeller in the family. Sloan tends to be at a loss for words. I chuck my dinner and go upstairs to my room. I am beyond pissed. Why can't these boys make good choices? While I don't drink, Sloan has a beer now and again. They know both their grandfathers and uncles had been alcoholics. It's not like we perpetuate this party atmosphere and encourage use. I hear Jackson outside crying to Sloan. I look out the window and Joey is in the back yard. Sloan comes upstairs and says Jackson is so emotional. We ask Carson what he knows. He says he thinks Jackson drank pure moonshine. *Really?* Jackson comes to me and apologizes and says he doesn't want to disappoint us and that he is homesick and doesn't think he wants to go back to college. I just tell him we'll talk about it tomorrow. He asks if Joey can stay over. They are just going to watch movies.

About 11:30 p.m., Sloan's phone dings. I get up to look at it and there is a message from our cell provider stating that someone from our house or account has called 911.

Leaning over the banister, I scream "Jackson, are you messing around with 911?!" No response.

I run downstairs and Jackson is talking to 911 dispatch and rubbing Joey's chest. Joey is gray and gasping for air.

I scream for Sloan, and Carson comes out of his room. EMTs and police come into the house. They lay Joey on the ground and put the bag over his mouth to help him breathe.

"Son, what did your friend take?"

Jackson hesitates.

"This is not a time to lie, Jackson, just tell them."

He tells the EMTs that it's heroin.

Apparently, Joey went into the bathroom when Jackson and Maddie, Jackson's girlfriend, walked out to her car. When he came back in, Joey was sitting on the couch in the dark. Jackson started having a conversation about the movie, when Joey didn't say anything Jackson turned on the light and Joey wasn't breathing. I start thinking to myself is this why Jackson vomited all over the porch? Had Jackson and Joey been doing heroin?!

I call Joey's mom and tell her what is going on and she says, "Are you sure he's not having a seizure? Joey has had some seizures lately."

The EMT says it is not a seizure, that he is overdosing on heroin. They are taking him to the hospital. After everyone leaves, Sloan, the boys, and I stand in the living room viewing the aftermath. I turn and look at the boys and say the opiate epidemic has just infiltrated our home. We all are in shock.

Over the next week, I call several recommended psychologists and a psychiatrist. Only one out of the many I called are taking new patients. They all listen to our story and all say we are doing what needs to be done to intervene. "Good luck," they say.

Finally, a recommended therapist who writes books and speaks on adolescent addiction takes Carson on as a patient. Only appointment times are 8:00 a.m. This will have to work. He starts school at 9:00 a.m. He'll be late a couple times a week. Carson goes begrudgingly. He tells me she is too nice and that he can bamboozle her. I tell the therapist this and we continue with the appointments. There are appointments that he just refused to go to. He's too tired. He has to study. If I reschedule and we get an afterschool time, he'll text me at the last minute saying he has to stay after school. The appointments cost $125.00, whether he goes or not.

8.

Having one "How can she stand it?" thing happen does not protect you from more things happening...the hard truth is: There is no quota.

Joan Wickersham

For some reason, the kids had a day off during the week a couple weeks before Thanksgiving. Carson comes home from school late the day before their off day, and I can tell immediately that he is on something.

"Carson, are you high?"

"No, don't be silly."

He comes over and hugs on me and tells me he is so sad because he just wants to be with his girlfriend, that he loves her and wants to take her on dates and not just to have sex. He weeps as I hug him, and I notice I can feel his ribs. Carson had just started dating this girl from school who seems to have grabbed his heart. I feel that the relationship is very one-sided.

A friend of his shows up at our house unexpectedly as Carson is having this very emotional moment. They are going to go get vape juice, another epidemic amongst teens. Carson grabs his keys, and we say that he cannot drive. He doesn't fight it. His friend shrugs and gives us a look like, "I don't know what's up with Carson."

They are gone fifteen minutes and he's back home and back in his room. He sleeps the next day to nearly 3:00 p.m. I go into his room, and I give him a story saying he has a doctor's appointment Friday. I tell him I am concerned about his weight loss.

I say, "let's go see what you weigh." He weighs 137 at six feet tall. I call the doctor's office and talk to her nurse.

"What was Carson's weight in June at his well-check?" She says 159. She and I have a conversation about the fact that I think he is using, and she says they'll do bloodwork to look for anything wrong health-wise and they'll do a drug screen. He won't know. I have got to keep this appointment as no big deal otherwise he might not go.

It's Thanksgiving week and on Monday the nurse calls with the results of the blood test. He tested positive for opiates, particularly Percocet. I go into his room and take his keys and tell him he is grounded. He tries to tell me that he was at his friend's house and he had a migraine, and the friend gave him a 10 mg or something of the sort.

I want to believe him, but I know in my heart that he is lying.

Jackson comes home from college on Wednesday and he and his girlfriend take the car and go out, but they don't get back until 11:00 p.m. Around 12:30 a.m. Sloan's "find a friend" alert goes off. Carson has left the house and is in a shady part of town. I run downstairs and ask Jackson and Maddie where he went. I said he is not supposed to be driving. They said he came out of his room when they got home, asked for the keys and said he was going to find some weed. I call him, he answers, and I tell him to get his ass home. Around 2:00 a.m. I get up to go to the restroom. I walk into the living room and Carson is passed out on the couch, halfway between sitting up and lying down. Jackson is watching TV. I just look at him and say, "I'm done! You take care of him."

On Thanksgiving Day, we have twenty-seven people coming over to celebrate. Carson wakes early and it is apparent that he did not go get pot the night before, but he purchased Xanax. Again! The effects of Xan bars on him (and I would think for most users) causes him to have an exaggerated gait, a hooded look, and he is agitated, sometimes even aggressive. It has caused him to have blackouts. He does not sleep or eat or take in fluids. It also causes him to seek some other substance to keep him high longer.

As we are icing up the coolers of beer and pop, Carson starts to sneak beers. People are arriving and Sloan and I are doing everything possible to make everything seem A-OK. Carson is obviously under the influence and grandparents are noticing, while the cousins are trying to contain him. Aunts are asking if he is OK. At one point, I see Carson sneak another beer and go into the bathroom. I jump up from the table and excuse myself from the conversation. I go into the bathroom, and Carson is like "What the hell, Mom?"

"Give me that beer, right now. No more!"

"Fine, fine, what is your problem?" he says to me.

The next evening, we were to host my side of the family. I text my cousin and explain to her what happened on Thanksgiving. "Not sure we should have the kids witness Carson like this. He's better, but I can tell it'll be a couple days before he is normal." We decide to go ahead and have everyone over for pizza and games.

Carson participates, but thirteen-year-olds Megan and April start to ask their moms what's wrong with Carson. Sloan and I are just exhausted.

After everyone leaves, I go into Carson's room and he is a wreck. His girlfriend is breaking up with him. I guess she got wind of him taking Xans after they were together the night before Thanksgiving. Sloan and I had let Carson go ice skating with her even though he was grounded. We find ourselves supporting "good behavior" over and over, and now we know it is to his detriment. You want to encourage good choices. We feel that praise and reward for good grades, playing well in sports, and good decisions will keep him from making bad choices. It's psychology 101, right?

The next day he is back to normal; he must have only taken one dose. He is miserable because of the girlfriend. I call Fairbanks and talk to them about the blood test and him being high even though he knew there were going to be a lot of people at his house. They suggest bringing him in for an assessment. I go down to his room and see his best friend has come to check in on him. This friend is like family, we've taken him everywhere with us. He has seen the good, bad, and ugly of our family. I sit down and ask Carson to go back to Fairbanks. He immediately starts to cry hysterically and says he can't do it. He says he'll keep seeing his therapist and won't use. He's learned his lesson with losing the girlfriend. His best friend and I exchange looks. I can tell I won't get anywhere with him in this emotional state. I let it go.

Between Thanksgiving and Christmas, life is relatively quiet. Carson goes to therapy appointments, and he finishes the semester well. Christmas Eve Day is quiet; Sloan is working, Jackson is finishing shopping, and Carson is in his room.

I tell Carson that I'm going to go lay down for about a half hour before getting ready for church. Sloan and Jackson come home and we all finish getting ready. We pile in the car and Carson starts to become chatty. Sloan and I give each other a sideways glance, knowing this is unlike him. Jackson is the chatty one. Carson seems really "up." I am trying not to freak out. We run into church late and squeeze into the pew with friends. As service goes on, Carson's behavior starts to become peculiar: loud talking, fidgety, he doodles on the giving envelopes. Our friends and their kids keep glancing over. Service ends, and we say our quick goodbyes because we have to get him out of there.

We head to my mother-in-law's, where Sloan's brother and family are meeting us for Christmas Eve dinner and gifts. Carson is overly gregarious. He has become the life of the party. My sister-in-law knows . . . she has gone through this before. Her family has been riddled with addiction. She gives me compassionate looks.

We all are just trying to get through the evening without Grandma and Aunt Nana catching on. At one point Carson disappears into the bathroom for so long, Sloan has to pull him out. He claims he was vaping. We head home.

"Carson, you are high."

"No, I'm not."

Jackson says, "Dude, seriously."

We walk through the door and Carson goes straight to his bedroom and vomits in his waste basket. Carson never throws up.

"Carson, what did you take?"

He's now acting like he is drunk and weepy. "I drank some alcohol." Sloan comes around the corner and asked where he got it from because no one was drinking at Grandma's. He tells us he drank isopropyl alcohol.

The pattern of his binge is to keep a high going. Carson becomes melancholy and says that he's ruining Christmas and that he doesn't deserve to be part of this family. Whatever he took is not his usual M.O. We are scared. I get him tucked into bed and I climb in with him. Throughout the night he moans and groans. He cries in his sleep. Carson sleeps through Christmas Day except for opening presents. I try to keep things normal. Grandma and Nana come over for brunch, but Carson goes back to bed. He sleeps through until I wake him to go to Fairbanks for an assessment on the twenty-sixth. He's groggy, yet nervous . . . he doesn't fight me.

We get to Fairbanks and check in. Dylan, a counselor from his first stint in Fairbanks, greets him and says, "Carson, Carson, Carson . . . " I can tell that Carson is relieved that it's Dylan. Carson agrees to start intensive outpatient after New Year's.

However, three days later, Carson snuck out or had drugs delivered to him. It seems that drug dealers are like pizza delivery people these days. There have been a number of times where Sloan has had to pull Carson out of a dealer's car after we have gone to bed.

It's Sunday morning and we are to have my parents over to celebrate Christmas. As Sloan and I are having coffee and discussing everything that has transpired since Labor Day, we are in a state of shock. We hash over a few times that we thought he was high, and he was adamant he was not. Like when we went on a college visit and he was so hyper, overly inquisitive, inappropriately interrupting, to the point that we were getting looks.

"Are we crazy?" I say to Sloan.

I decide to sneak into Carson's bedroom to grab his phone. I am curious if I can see where he is getting these drugs. I remember his passcode and can't believe he hasn't changed it.

What I learn is absolutely heartbreaking.

Even though texts or chats are in their slang and coded, I can tell it's no good. I hide his phone and find his iPad and stash it. We have to do something. Carson wakes up and it is obvious that he acquired something the night before. He is hotter than a cat on a hot tin roof, and he's rummaging through drawers, looking in closets.

"Carson, what are you looking for?"

Through that hooded look we know so well, he says quite explicitly, "You very well know what I am looking for!"

"Carson, you no longer have access to your phone or iPad. It is clear you snuck out and got high last night, even though three days ago you agreed to start IOP, again."

He starts throwing things and screaming in my face. I walk upstairs to get away from him, and Sloan follows him around the house keeping him from following me. Carson starts to pack his huge football bag with clothes and food. He says he isn't living here anymore. Sloan says nothing. Carson grabs his skateboard and bag and leaves the house. We let him go. When does rock bottom become rock bottom? It sure seems like it's our rock bottom.

I call my dad to cancel our dinner and tell him everything. He is concerned that Carson is becoming more aggressive, bordering on violent. He is worried for me and my safety. I am hysterical now. I am at my breaking point. Sloan is, too.

Carson returns home about seven hours later. He is high, but more like he smoked weed. He realized he has no place to go. His druggie friends can't take him in, and his best friends probably don't know about this latest binge. He "relinquishes" and says he'll start IOP. I feel this extreme sadness, as if the physical exhaustion is weighing on my soul.

Carson spends the next couple of days in his room watching movies and playing video games. He is very quiet. He agrees to go to a movie on New Year's Eve with Sloan, Jackson, and me. He's with us but is absent. After the movie

I ask everyone if they want to stop into the Foley's for our usual New Year's plans. No one is up to it. I want something that seems normal. Carson feels so much shame, I can see it seeping from his pores. He knows I talk to Auntie Mern, and he's afraid of the judgment. Even though I tell him so many people love him, and that they are concerned, he doesn't believe me.

The next day, he calls me into his room and tearfully tells me he cannot go to IOP. He will miss baseball conditioning, and everyone will know why, and they'll judge him. I try to convince him otherwise, because in March he turns eighteen and we won't be able to force him into rehab. He says he'll hit baseball hard and work on his academics. He'll start going to NA meetings. We go with him to his first meeting that night. We agree with his plan.

We've learned that if recovery is to be successful the addict has to drive the train, right?

9.

...Jesus wept

~John 11:35 (NIV)
[or Rev 21:4]

February rolled around, and we found ourselves attending two funerals within weeks of each other. An elementary classmate of Carson's was found dead at his grandparent's house. It came out later that it was an accidental overdose. The family didn't know that he had a substance use issue till the toxicology came back months later. I tell Carson what we are about to walk into is a parent's worst nightmare!

"I know, Mom."

"Please, Carson, I beg you to stop."

With his head down, he says, "I will, Mom."

The sanctuary was packed with families, coaches, teachers, administrators, large groups of teenagers— practically standing room only. As the family came in, I watched the young man's mom walk down the aisle with our pastor and my heart ached so painfully that I thought I was having a heart attack. I prayed to God for her strength but most of all for Carson to be moved, to be changed, to be saved.

A week or so later, on a Saturday morning, Carson texted me from his friend's house where he had spent the night. "Mom, you need to call Joey's mom."

I texted back, "Why?"

"People on Snapchat say that Joey is dead."

"What?!"

Jackson is home for the weekend, and I go into his room. "Jackson, wake up . . . I need to tell you something." He groggily turns over. "Carson just texted me that a rumor is going around that Joey has passed."

He sits up and grabs his phone and starts typing away. I go into my room and call some moms who might know because their daughters are friends with Joey, one being Carson's best friend's mom. They don't know anything but are calling their daughters at their colleges. Sloan and I decide I need to call Joey's mom, Kelly. I don't want to alarm her if it's just a rumor, but after what happened to him at our house back in September, I'm scared. I ring Kelly's cell phone . . .

"Hello, Dawn, it's Sarah." Sarah is a mutual friend, and Kelly's best friend.

"Oh my God, it's true? Is Joey dead?" Sloan begins to sob as he sits next to me.

"Yes, he was found early this morning. He had aspirated."

As Sarah tells me a few more details, tears roll down my face. I don't know if I can stand much more.

I feel like I'm in the middle of a war with casualties all around.

I call back Carson's best friend's mom, and she knows from her daughter. We decide to go where the boys are to confirm the news and make sure they are OK. I personally want them to know so maybe, just maybe, Carson and his friends will be scared shitless, anything to stop their foolish experimentations.

As I stand before these boys and proclaim the severity of the situation, Karin and I tell them how much we love them. They are good kids, smart, talented, athletic, with loving hearts! But knowing what we've been through with Carson and what had happened to Joey at our house, they need to know that this is serious shit. Carson just sobs in Karin's arms as the others have a sad and yet "deer in headlights look." Maybe this is the turning point!

By the end of the week, Jackson comes home for Joey's funeral. He and Sarah's boy, Drew, are going to speak. Jackson seems to be OK, but I am not too sure. All Carson's friends are taking off school to go, along with several of their parents. My heart aches as we enter to find our seats. The place is packed, like last week's funeral. This is not normal. People so young should not be dying, especially by drug overdoses. Usually, we celebrate a life well-lived, but these kids haven't had a chance to live yet.

Sarah's boy speaks about Joey being his best friend and that living without him will be hard. You can see the anguish in his demeanor. Jackson tells some funny stories about Joey. The pastor speaks about how very sensitive Joey was and how his empathy was like a sponge. He felt whatever his friends or family were feeling.

Rest in Peace, sweet Joey.

10.

The science is indisputable: addiction is a chronic disease that changes the brain.

Shatterproof.org

Carson's baseball season starts. We are all busy. He's at practice or games every night and most Saturdays. I'm team mom and have been for years. Sloan and I go to every game. We love watching Carson and all his athleticism. Sloan and I say all the time, "When he is 'good,' he is so good, and when he is 'bad,' he is so bad."

For the last couple of years, there hasn't been an in-between. We are constantly chasing him to be good, productive, "on the straight and narrow," and out of harm's way. Our mantra is "get him through high school," and then we'll be able to breathe a little easier.

The Monday after his last regular season game, Carson skips school to go sell plasma to buy some weed. He probably thought he deserved it. He'd been "good" since January. Instead of buying weed he saw on Snapchat, "Bars for sale." He couldn't resist. He spent the whole week off school and high. I just kept calling in to school saying he was sick until Thursday, when he woke up and was still "not right." I had to call the principal and assistant principal because we were going into Memorial Day weekend.

On Memorial Day, sectionals were starting and then Tuesday, Carson was to leave on a four-day all-grade field trip. They have been through this with us before. It's time to come clean. I get a hold of the assistant principal on his cell phone.

"Jacob?" I start to cry. I have been holding it together all week as I worked on clients and tried to keep Carson home and calm. I was waiting until the "storm" passed. However, this time around he was hyper-focused on me, and everything I did was wrong.

"Jacob, Carson has started using again."

He says, "Oh, Dawn, I am so sorry. First and foremost, this is not your fault, and you and Sloan need to get to an Al-Anon meeting." Jacob has family who struggle with addiction. He knows how this all "works." He says I need to call him Monday night after sectionals and let him know if Carson is back to "normal." He feels if we can get him out of the city and some days clean, we all can intervene. Jacob's compassion is hard to take. I guess I was expecting him to say, "Tough, he is suspended." Not because Jacob would be mean, but because there are rules and he has to administer those rules.

Later that day after I get done with clients, I sit down to breathe for a minute. Carson comes in and starts to berate me. Sloan walks in from work to witness the volley. I get up. I have had enough. I walk downstairs to do laundry, just to do something to get away from him. He follows me, and I tell him he needs to leave me alone. He can't stop. I just break down sobbing, and I have this overwhelming need to leave.

As I push past Sloan and Carson on the stairs, I walk up to my bedroom and start packing a bag. Sloan is saying, "You can't leave," while Carson is saying, "No, Mom, I'll leave."

Through deep sobs, I leave. I start to drive. I need a break. I am broken.

I find my way to a hotel; I just need to have quiet and honestly, I need Sloan to sort Carson out. I have dinner at my childhood best friend's house. I talk a little about this latest relapse or binge. In the end they let me just be. I can see their empathy on their face. They want to fix "it." A lot of people want to help fix "it." They can't imagine what we are going through, though through the years of friendship they feel my deep sorrow.

The next morning, I get up to do errands. Finally, later in the day, Carson calls. "Mom, you've got to come home. Dad is miserable without you. I'll leave."

"Carson, you can't. You have no money. Where would you possibly go?"

"I'll be home later."

He sounds a bit back to normal. I get home, and he is remorseful. He says he's going to Uber to a meeting at Fairbanks.

Memorial Day weekend is a big weekend in Indianapolis. We host the Indianapolis 500, the world's largest sporting event. Our family, like most here in Indy, make the whole weekend full of activities, very much a party atmosphere. Sloan and his brothers have been going to the race for years and when the kids turned about thirteen, they started going, too. We have race pools that the teens love to be a part of.

Everyone meets at our house to pack lunches and decide which route they are taking to their parking spot. The excitement is contagious.

However, I realize later in the day that I forgot to check Carson's cooler for beer.

The day rolls on and they send me pictures of an awesome day. Jackson texts me that Carson has won the pool, which is $110.00. Shit! They all arrive back to our house where some stay for a cookout. Sloan asks if we should let Carson keep the money. We make the suggestion to save his money for the field trip Tuesday. He says he will, he's just taking $30 and go buy vape pods for the week. He takes off into the village.

Race day is exhausting: being in the sun, navigating crowds, drinking beer. We all crash early; baseball sectionals start in the morning. Carson needs to be at the diamonds by 8:30 a.m.

I go into wake him around 7:30 a.m. and on his nightstand is an empty dab cartridge. These cartridges are small attachments pre-filled with cannabis concentrate that are used on vape pens. The average THC potency is between 70% and 90%, compared to an average of 18% in a joint (Marijuanabreak.com). A dab cartridge is not something you consume in a "nighter of partying." It is highly psychoactive.

"Carson, wake up, you need to get into the shower, you need to be at the diamonds in an hour."

He moans and groans, but he gets up.

While he is getting ready, I tell Sloan what I found, and we aren't sure we should let him play. We can't tell yet what the lasting effects of consuming an entire dab will have on him. He comes out of his room and as always when he is using, his right eye is turned in slightly. His gait is off, again. He packs his gear and says to me, "Let's go." I drive him to the diamonds and walk in with him. I tell his coach that I am not sure if he is in good shape for the game. I desperately wanted Coach to get the hint.

Carson and the pitcher go into the bullpen to warm up. Carson can catch, but he cannot throw straight at all. I leave and hope for the best.

Sloan and I arrive back at the diamonds in time for the first pitch. As the game goes on, Carson overthrows, underthrows, or throws crooked. Parents start to say, "Wow, is Carson not feeling well?" Sloan has to get up and walk because it is painful to watch. I mumble something like he'd been sick all week and went to the race yesterday. I get up and look into the dugout after Coach pulls him during inning 5.

I overhear one of his friends say to another, "Is he high or what?!" The other players must know. How can they not? Despite Carson not being at the top of his game, the team pulled off a close game against a much bigger school. In the end we lost by two. Everyone heads to the coach's house for the year-end cookout.

As we enjoy a day at the coach's house with food, games, and awards, Carson starts to act normal. I sit and chat with one of the assistant coaches. He mentions that Carson's game was off, and I am compelled to tell him that Carson struggles with substance abuse, and we have had a bad weekend.

The coach looks at me with that look like, "Really, Carson?!"

It wasn't the time to get into our story over the past couple of years, but I said, "Yeah, it's been a rough journey and we aren't done yet." He pats my hand and wishes us all the luck. I wish luck could fix this unending cycle.

I call the assistant principal, Jacob, Monday night and tell him that Carson played in sectionals. I left out that he was "hung over." We needed him to go on this field trip. He needed several days without any substances. We needed the binge cycle to break.

As the week wore on, Jackson received a text from one of Carson's friends who was on the trip. They think he brought something with him. I questioned why they would think that. Jackson shows me a picture of Carson stripping down to his underwear and running into Lake Michigan amongst a group of girls and guys. He was the only one doing this. Jackson continued to show me a video Carson made of himself with other students in downtown Chicago. Yep. We can always tell by his eyes.

Friday evening, I picked him up on return from the field trip, and he seemed fine. Maybe he wasn't on anything all week. We all are just so paranoid; we just don't know what the truth is when it comes to his use.

The weekend goes by fairly smoothly. Hopefully, we are through the cycle. Because Carson had lost his car privileges, someone gave him a ride home from school Monday.

He comes through the door and out back to get his bike. He says he needs to go buy vape pods for some kids at school. He comes home, eats dinner, and goes to his room.

Around 9:00 p.m., Sloan and I are getting ready for the next day. I go into Carson's room because I hadn't heard from him in a while. He is passed out on his bed with his feet dangling over.

"Sloan!!!!"

I start to smack Carson's face, calling his name. After about thirty seconds, he grabs my wrist to stop me.

"Carson, what did you take?"

He says nothing, just that he fell asleep. He gets up and walks into the kitchen, asking what is for dessert. Sloan sees something hanging out from underneath his shorts. "Carson, what do you have in your shorts?"

He wriggles his shorts around like he's drunk and says nothing. Sloan pounces on Carson and starts to wrestle him for what is in his underpants. Carson gets a burst of energy and headbutts Sloan into the refrigerator, knocking him down. Carson runs to his room and slams the door. Sloan busts through into his room screaming he is not letting him take what he has. I scream for Jackson who had been upstairs in his room sleeping.

Jackson runs down the stairs and together they are wrestling Carson on his bed. Three large guys in a small room, furniture was tipping over, lamps were crashing, they were headed toward the hall. I ran out the front door and called 911 from the front lawn.

Sloan is out of breath as he comes outside and hands me six or eight pills wrapped in a tissue. Jackson walks out the side door with no shirt or shoes and takes off down the block. I yell, "Where are you going?!"

Jackson yells back, "I am not sticking around to watch my brother get arrested!"

The police arrive. It's Officer O'Conner.

"Thank God, Michael, it's you who came."

"Where is he?"

I point toward Carson's room. A few minutes later, they all come into the kitchen, and I show Officer O'Conner the pills we took off Carson. I was able to look up the number on the pills and they were barbiturates of some kind.

Officer O'Conner discusses with Carson his options. He washes the pills down the sink, runs the disposal, and says, "This is your last chance, Carson. You need to go back to rehab."

Carson is adamant he is not going. He is high; he can't make any decisions right now. As he leans against the counter, he can't even stand straight. Officer O'Conner is starting to lose his patience. "Carson, it's back to Fairbanks or jail."

Carson puts his hands out to be handcuffed. The other officer calls for the paddy wagon, and we walk outside. As Carson sits on the stoop, I can't help but be disgusted and devastated at the same time. I ask him if he realizes that he is eighteen and will be going to "big boy" jail? He's so out of it, he doesn't care. Officer O'Conner begins to tell us that he lost his brother to drug addiction and ultimately drug overdose. He seems as distraught as we are. The paddy wagon pulls up, and Sloan and I let him go. Will this be his "rock bottom" now?

The next day, we get a call from Marion County Jail. "Mom, OK, you can get me out now." I can tell he is still under the influence. We don't say much . . . what can we say that he'll heed any advice from? We have got to let him sweat it out. He will eventually get in front of a judge with a public defender and be arraigned.

The next morning, I call a friend who works for attorneys downtown and tell her what has happened. She tells me she'll look into it and get back to me. About an hour later she calls, "Girl, it's time to get a criminal defense attorney." She says his charge was not a drug charge. It was an assault charge, Sloan being the victim. In these cases, the state takes over and prosecutes because of the domestic violence law. Carson is not allowed to come anywhere near Sloan, myself, or the house. He will be getting an ankle monitor. I hang my head and just beg God to make it stop. I call an attorney we have used before. Having boys, it's good to have a criminal defense attorney on speed dial. Like, what the fuck?!

We get a hold of Mr. Clifford. After we tell him everything we have been going through and the latest incident, he does some investigating of his own and calls to tell me that my girlfriend was correct. He has also found out that Carson has already been in front of a judge and is now somewhere between two holding facilities and the ankle monitoring place. Basically, he is lost in the system.

I haven't heard from my son in over twenty-four hours.

Mr. Clifford calls back in a couple hours and says he has found him but can't talk to him. They plan to release him that night. His third night of being in jail. The kicker is he can't come home. I call my parents and they say no. They are in their eighties and have money and medicines in the house. They are scared. I get it.

I call Carson's best friend's parents. They need to talk it over. Mr. Clifford calls back. His wife, who is connected to the addiction's community, is trying to get him in somewhere that night. No luck.

Finally, Carson calls. It's 10:00 p.m. and he is getting his ankle bracelet on. He's tearful. "I knew when you didn't show in court that I was on my own."

"Carson, we have hired Mr. Clifford, and you two are going back to court in the morning."

"But I have a public defender."

I tell him that it's OK, Mr. Clifford will sort it out. I tell him that he might have to walk over to the men's shelter when he is released.

Mr. Clifford calls back. I quickly tell Carson to hold on and switch over. Mr. Clifford tells me to get Jackson to pick him up and that we are going to break some rules, but it's a matter of safety. I am to go downtown and get a hotel room for the night and Jackson is to bring Carson to me. We are to meet him and Sloan at the courthouse the next morning. I switch back over and tell Carson that Jackson will be waiting for him.

I meet the boys in the lobby, and Carson, again, looks broken. He is wearing basketball shorts that are falling off of him, he is stooped over, dirty and greasy. I just embrace him.

We say goodbye to Jackson and head up to our room. He goes into the bathroom and locks the door.

"Carson, please do not lock the door."

He unlocks it and gets into the shower without saying a word. He's in there for about thirty minutes.

He has a snack, crawls into bed and passes out.

The next morning, he showers again, dresses, and we are on our way to court. We meet Sloan and Mr. Clifford in front of the courthouse and head up to the courtroom. Mr. Clifford talks to the prosecutor, and then they call Carson up so they all can talk with the Judge. I see Carson nodding his head. The prosecutor and the judge have agreed to drop the assault charge if Carson completes rehab over the summer. Carson signs paperwork and gets the ankle bracelet removed. Mr. Clifford has an appointment for Carson back at Fairbanks later that day.

Carson is starving so we get him pizza across from the courthouse. He is very contrite. He usually is after a crisis. He is remorseful and is gung-ho in getting sober.

We know the pattern now. Bender, crisis, remorse, rehab. Or the promise to do meetings or rehab. This time he is going. I have hope. This is it. I know it is. This will work!

11.

*Addiction is a public health crisis.
Overdose is the #1 cause of accidental
death in the United States. Every
four minutes a parent loses a child to
addiction.*

Shatterproof.org

Carson spends twenty-one days in residential inpatient and then another ten days in partial hospitalization. He then starts intensive outpatient, which will be six weeks.

Within the time he is in inpatient, he misses out on family vacation. I had booked a cottage on the lake my grandparents had loved so I could spread my mom's ashes. It's sad that Carson missed out on yet another family event. I wish he had been with us.

It hits home what it means when the term "consequences of addiction" is used. Like when making choices, there are good ones and bad ones. With substance abuse, the consequences are always negative. I know that no one wants to be an addict. Carson did not choose to be. He unlocked the part of the brain that is the reward center and with his age and because of the gene pool he comes from, he has unleashed a monster.

As programming continues, he makes progress. He has admitted that he is an addict. He has come to the realization that school is a source of anxiety. We make an appointment and meet with the assistant principal, social worker, and academic counselor. They are supportive, understanding, and helpful. Carson runs the meeting and is very forthright with everything that has gone on. He promises to go to the social worker's office when he starts feeling overwhelmed. The assistant principal makes Carson a new schedule. He does not need to finish the diploma portion of IB (International Baccalaureate). For his senior year, he needs English 12 both semesters and one semester of math. This will still allow him to go to college if he so chooses. Carson will be going every other day. On his off days he plans to go to meetings and work. We are on a roll! Life is good!

As Carson's IOP starts to finish up, we see a change in his demeanor. He seems depressed. He doubts whether he can say no to using. He's lost his drive. His counselor is concerned. He promises he will continue with meetings, and he will check in with her once a week for the next twelve weeks. The last night of IOP, Carson comes home happy and says he's going to chill and do homework, since he has school the next day. Late that night, I wake to a ding announcement on my phone. The security camera has gone off. I check the video. Carson is walking the bike down the driveway. I run downstairs and he's already gone. I call, and he answers, "What's up?"

"Carson, where are you going? It's one in the morning and you have school."

"I'm just riding to see a friend."

"What friend, where are you?"

"I'm by the skate park."

"Carson, get home now! Don't you remember the bike's front tire goes flat?"

"OKKKKK, I'll turn around, just chill, Mom."

I sit in the backyard and wait. Fifteen minutes goes by and no sign of him. I grab my keys and jump in the car. As I'm heading toward the park, I call. "I'm coming to get you. Send me your location."

He hangs up but sends his location. I pull onto the street, still not sure what house. I call again. "You had better come out now or I am calling the police. I am sure that the parents of this kid do not want to wake up to police pounding on their door."

He comes out and puts his bike in the car. "Carson, are you high?"

"I just took a hit or two of a joint."

I am in shock.

The next morning, he gets up. As he heads out the door, we have a few words. He leaves, and I stood, watching after him, wondering if he's still high. I go through my day waiting for a call from school. Jackson texts me later in the day to tell me Carson's friends are texting him saying Carson is high at school. I text Carson and tell him to come straight home after school. He asks why. So as not to give up his friends, I tell him a teacher called me and told me he was acting strange. I meet him at the door when he arrives, and my fears are confirmed. I open the door to that familiar hooded look. As he pushes past, he is mumbling something about his friend and is bitching up a storm. I hear him in the bathroom just raking his friend up one side and down the other. Carson is threatening him. I text the friend and say, "Hang up on him." I tell the friend he does not need to put up with Carson. He obviously is and has been high. I text, "it's OK to put limits and boundaries on your relationship." The friend texts back and says thank you and sorry.

I am too.

A little while later, Carson's best friend calls. "Mrs. McCord, Carson said you drug tested him, and it was just pot."

"No, honey, unfortunately he is lying."

I explain what happened the night before, but that now I am sure he has taken Xans. I tell him it's time to put limits and boundaries on their relationship, too. I can tell he is devastated that Carson lied to him.

Carson comes into the porch. "Who are you talking to.?!" I hang up with his friend and say no one. Sloan walks in from work and once again witnesses Carson and me having words. Because Sloan gets up at 4:30 a.m. every morning, I did not wake him the night before, so he is clueless to what has happened in the last twenty-four hours. He is quickly catching on. Sloan's shoulders just sag.

After an evening of Carson following me around and trying to engage me in banter, and me responding by repeating, "Carson, leave me alone and go to your room," he finally goes to sleep.

The next morning, he wakes early and comes to talk to me. He is remorseful. Through his tears, he explains that he had found one Xan a couple of weeks ago and that he saved it. This makes sense in the timeline of when he started to get depressed and his resolve started to wane. "Mom, I thought I could handle it."

I calmly say, "Carson, you know oh so well that relapse starts well before you actually use."

"I know . . . I'm going to call my IOP counselor today and go to a meeting."

After sixty days of being sober, or so I thought, he starts over. Everything we have learned is that relapse is a part of recovery. But how many times? How long will we have to keep going through this? I keep telling myself, "I just need to get him through high school, then he is on his own." It's just August of his senior year.

A couple weeks later, Sloan and I leave Carson sitting at the dining room table working on homework and run errands. When we arrive home, Carson is still sitting at the table and he is in a tither. He feels like he is not understanding the material and that his essay is pure "bullshit." He says he is going to go take a shower. Thirty minutes later he comes into the living room, plops down in the chair, and starts to cry. "I think I just had a panic attack in the shower."

He explains that his anxiety had been building and that he thought if he took a shower, it would get better. "Do you want a hug?" He comes over to me and just sobs in my arms. "Carson, I have read about anxiety and depression and substance use. I think it's time to talk to the doctor. She can get you into a psychiatrist."

He agrees. I latch onto any morsel of change he exhibits. It makes me feel that he is progressing. It gives me hope.

On the first of September, a friend tells me that a daughter of a neighbor of hers is doing a study at our local children's hospital. It's about adolescence, addiction, and dual diagnosis. I call to get Carson in for an evaluation. They accept him into the program. He meets with a grad student weekly, which includes drug testing. Over the next couple of appointments, they continue testing and therapy. The study is so full that the soonest he can see the psychiatrist to talk about med management is the first of November.

Carson seems to be trying. He goes to school every other day, goes to therapy every Tuesday, checks in at Fairbanks on Wednesdays, works about fifteen hours a week, and goes to an NA meeting on Fridays. He passes drug tests. All's good!

Until it's not.

Carson's psychologist calls around the first of October after Carson had just been to see her. He has failed his drug test. He tested positive for opiates, cocaine, and THC. Carson had gone to work after his appointment, so we don't talk to him till 9:00 p.m. that night. He comes home knowing we already know. He makes no excuses. He doesn't seem like he is giving up. He says he's going to be truthful with Sarah, his IOP counselor at Fairbanks. We are calm yet concerned. He tells us not to worry. He has to "do this." It's his path.

Over the next week and a half, we are pretty sure something is brewing. We know the pattern. There are times his eyes are not right. He still goes to his meetings, therapy, and work. School is now on fall break. After the failed drug test, we took the car away, again. He can use it for his responsibilities only.

He comes home to trade out the car for the bike. There are hours of time he goes missing. He always has a story. I check up a couple of times. He says he is with friends that we would allow, but he is not. He sends me pictures of him going into work or meetings. I check to see if he arrived at his psychology appointment. He starts hanging out at the Legion. We ask why. He gives us some story that he is accepted over there and that he has fun.

Really?! A bunch of old vets sitting at the bar. He sends pictures of him singing karaoke to a few people.

October 18, 2019, Carson overdoses on heroin.

12.

One in three families are impacted by substance use disorder.

SAMHSA.gov

Only one in ten seek treatment for substance use.

Center for Behavioral Health Statistics
and Quality

We walk the back halls following Carson as the medical staff move him to ICU. The ICU staff ask Sloan and me to step out as they get him settled. When we are allowed back in the room, Carson has a huge oxygen mask on. This is the first step before intubation. He is still tied to the bed and they have given him another sedative to calm him down.

The ICU doctor calls for a neurology consult to figure out why he can't understand when we talk. A radiologist technician then comes in to take an ultrasound of his heart.

As Carson sleeps, we sit next to his bedside and watch the monitor as his oxygen level changes and his blood pressure remains horribly low. By now, I have filled all our friends and family in. They continuously text asking what we need, and inquire if they should come over. We say no, not yet. But honestly, I wish someone would show up. Prayers answered, and my friends Michele and Suzanne find their way to us, and I just break down at the sight of them. Julie comes back after her shift to sit with Carson while Sloan and I get something to eat. As we are in the cafeteria, we miss more friends who are coming to support us.

We return the next morning, and Carson had a fretful night. The ICU doctor said that the neurologist did not find any reason why he could not hear, and that Carson responded to the doctor just fine. The nurse said she was conversing with him on a whiteboard. My cousin, an ICU nurse at another hospital, and her daughter came to visit, and she witnessed Carson being unable to hear female voices. The whiz that she is in googling, found that there is a phenomenon that makes a person who abuses opiates have hearing loss. I call Suzie, who is an audiologist, and she confirms this. She'll test him when he stabilizes. Other family come and go all day. My dad arrives, and he is at such a loss for words, he just stands at Carson's bedside and watches him sleep. Pastor Carolyn comes later in the day and lays a prayer blanket over him, and we pray over him. Carson wakes when Sloan's brother and his wife come to visit. Uncle Mark, who has struggled with addiction, has been a huge support to Carson and as he holds Carson's hand, they both cry. My heart aches watching this.

At some point, I run down to the cafeteria to grab drinks and snacks, and as I come around the corner, I meet my cousins Eric and Kelly in the hallway outside the locked ICU doors. I pull them into the family waiting area and as they sit on either side of me, listening intently to my telling of the last thirty-six hours, I start to cry. I can't get a coherent word out. They grab my hands, and Kelly says he needs something more than Fairbanks. She says she'll call her friend whose son just returned from a long-term substance abuse program.

The next day, Carson is moved out of ICU. We have established that he cannot hear female voices. He has cardiomyopathy and his injection fraction rate is at 35% (55% is normal). They won't release him until they slowly increase his new heart medication. We spend the day taking turns sitting with him while the other goes into the lobby to make calls to Fairbanks and the insurance company. We feel like we are scrambling. He cannot come home. In fact, we said that to him at the last counseling session when he finished IOP this last time. "If you start using again, Carson, you cannot live at home." Fairbanks is a thirty-day acute recovery hospital. This will make his third time. His counselors are fabulous. He has a rapport with them, but even they agree the program is not long enough.

Something must change. There is no other choice. If he comes home, he'll die.

Suzie has me talk to a friend from her church. She is a psychotherapist in town who has a daughter in a long-term program out of state. Sandi explains their story to me and how they got their daughter into Red Oak Recovery, the women's program called the Willows, in Asheville, North Carolina. I contact Red Oak. I explain our situation, and they take our insurance information to run benefits. I quickly find out that they are out of network and that it would be better to self-pay. Their program is ninety days, has a program for guys, and they do camping trips on the weekends, individual and group therapy every day, and they encourage the 12 Steps, and can manage his medicines. This place sounds like just what Carson needs. He has learned everything he can in a hospital setting, and it's time for different.

The admissions director explains that it will be $23,000 a month. What?! "Oh, we can't afford that!" He says they are available if we change our minds.

With keeping family and friends up to date on Carson, I now have a team to help in researching ninety-day-plus programs. My childhood friend Christina researches the West Coast since she lives in Seattle. My cousin Kelly researches the Midwest, and friend Maryjane takes the East coast. Carson is released from the hospital and we drive over to Fairbanks. Sarah is waiting.

"I think it's time for Naltrexone," Carson says to Sarah when we walk through the door.

Naltrexone, or Vivitrol, is an opioid blocker. This cancels out the effects the user is trying to achieve. They feel nothing. This is to help with cravings, as well.

Sarah agrees and we are escorted to a conference room where we discuss what's next. I look at Carson and say he can't come home. He knows. The insurance team starts the process. We pray authorization will come swiftly. Sarah asks what our plan is if authorization doesn't come through till the morning. I say this IS our plan. I guess we'll stay in a hotel. Everyone agrees that would be best. We can't take him home. I can't trust him. I don't trust ourselves. As much as he is ready to stop the cycle, addiction is manipulative, and it will manipulate him if he comes back to our home and the environment he overdosed in. We wait.

As Sloan, Carson, and I wait in the café area, I respond to texts of people asking how it's going. I call Sandi, Suzie's pychotherapist friend. "How do you afford to have your daughter at Red Oak? You have three other children."

She says, "You just do, there is no other choice. We have gone through all our savings."

Her daughter has been in North Carolina nine months now. Three months at Red Oak and now six months in sober living. Their goal is to keep her away and sober a year. My heart races and my stomach turns. I can't see what that looks like. I can't see how to afford it. I know it's what has to be done. We have to change his people, places, and things.

At 5:25 p.m., Carson is admitted into Fairbanks. Insurance has approved five days and will re-evaluate after that. Really?! He just overdosed and spent three days in the hospital two of which were in ICU! He has heart issues and hearing loss. I think we have a problem here! I'm frustrated, tired, hungry! Sarah says this is a common insurance practice. It's not right, but it happens. She says not to worry, they won't kick him out at day five. I feel the clock ticking!

Carson is reunited with Allison, his inpatient counselor. During our first meeting with her, she tells us that she cried when she heard of his overdose. She is determined to help him find a longer program. When Carson isn't in some type of therapy, he is sitting with Alison or his recovery coach, Matt, at the computer researching programs all over the country.

On the "outside," we, our team of family and friends, are doing the same. All the recommendations are given to me so I can call and talk insurance and finances. I spend time between clients and in the evenings calling. Once I have a program "vetted," I send it over to Carson to call and ask his questions. He's eighteen. He has to have buy-in if this is going to work. Some places he dinks because they are too fancy or too Christian or too much like a hospital or the programming is like Fairbanks. Some people have advised us to say to him, "Tough, we are paying for it, you go where we tell you." Yea, that doesn't work usually . . . ever . . . but especially when they are of age as a young adult. We are already on rehab time number three over which he had no choice. Fairbanks is the best for adolescence and young adult in our area, in the state, even. But the same is not working any longer. It has to be different to break this cycle.

In between working and researching programs, I am picking Carson up from Fairbanks for cardiology and audiology appointments. The cardiologist has increased one of his heart meds. His audiologist is my best friend, Suzie, and finally we meet her on a Sunday at her office. It's been ten days since his overdose.

She tests him. We hope that the hearing loss is getting better. She explains the test to us and with tears in her eyes she says, "Bud, you have a 70% high frequency sensorineural hearing loss." She pauses before saying, "We can work with that. I'm just grateful you are still with us."

I'm a mess. She fits him with an old pair of donated hearing aids and says we will look into getting some assistance from his school district since technically he's still in school. Carson is thrilled he can hear every word and not every other. Suzie recommends asking our ENT doctor friend to prescribe a round of steroids. Studies have shown that will help.

One day runs into another, and the clock is ticking. We haven't found another program yet, but our insurance keeps approving inpatient every five days. Carson has looked into therapeutic wilderness programs and asks me to look at the three he picked out. Holy cow! Utah, Colorado, and

Georgia. I come back with a place in Southern Indiana, though we think that this place is still too close. I talk with him about Red Oak in North Carolina, and since we have gotten over sticker shock, we apply. Let's just see what we can possibly work out. Our "team" with all their researching for us has figured out the cost of the long-term treatment programs and my cousin tells me we should look into doing a "GoFundMe" to help pay for the cost. I reply to her that Sloan will not go for it. He is so private.

"Dawn, people want to help, and you don't need a casserole, give them a chance to."

"Ok, I'll talk to Sloan." In the meantime, she talks with the rest of the family and they all decide to gift us money to help. Sloan and I are overwhelmed by their generosity . . . it's so humbling.

Red Oak has asked for his medical records from when he was in the hospital after the overdose. Within a couple days they come back with a denial. They are concerned about his heart and any strenuous activity. Carson did not like the place in Southern Indiana.

"Mom, it's just like Fairbanks but set in the woods," he informs me. He decides to fill out the applications to Evoke in Utah, which was on my friend Christina's list, Open Sky in Colorado, and Blue Ridge Therapeutic Wilderness in Georgia. Carson does his part, and I call and talk to the admissions counselors in those programs. They all want to see his medical records from the overdose.

I get a letter from the cardiologist stating Carson is able to participate in these programs. Open Sky declines him. I am just waiting for Utah and Georgia to do the same. I'm frantic. Suzie tells me to ask for another injection fraction test. I speak out loud, "Would anything have changed? It's not even been a month."

Suzie says, "You have nothing to lose. He is a young, athletic, healthy boy. He has been on meds and has rested. Get the test!"

I call the cardiologist office and beg for another test and ask if we can get it as soon as possible. Soonest is a Saturday morning when we are to be in family group at Fairbanks. Alison lets him go early and we run to the heart hospital and he has the test. Now we wait. Alison calls and tells us that insurance is moving him to partial hospitalization. "What?! He can't come home, Alison!"

She knows this. "You can self-pay for night support. It's $80.00 a night." Of course, we say we'll pay.

Sloan has agreed to let me create a Plumfund and share our story on Facebook. Before I click post, I read to Sloan what I wrote:

To all our family and friends, near and far....it pains us to put this out there...our business, our secrets, our private life...why? Because, it's not pretty...it's not a praise or a brag about achievements...it's ugly, it's dirty and we are devastated. Carson has struggled with substance use since he was 16…what started as typical teenage experimenting, slowly turned into regular use. He has been in rehab and therapy 3 times. He works recovery but can't seem to "shake that monkey off his back." Sending him away will get him away from his environment and into a longer treatment program. 70-90 days inpatient then sober living for 6-9 months. The cost is high, insurance covers a fraction if any.… here's the kicker…it might not work…he's 18 years old…he's an addict.…but we have to give him a fighting chance. What else is the alternative? Please don't feel any pressure to give… but do pray for him and us! Love, Dawn and Sloan

I looked over at Sloan and tears just streamed down his face. Tears were streaming down mine. We cry a lot and often. I continued on and read him the statement on Plumfund:

My dear family and friends, it's with a very heavy heart that Sloan and I tell you that our Carson has struggled with substance abuse. On October 18th, Sloan found Carson unresponsive and gasping for breaths, our worst nightmare, he was overdosing. Carson is in a local short-term program but needs a longer-term program with sober living to give him a better chance of survival. Our insurance is quickly approaching max out and we have to go self-pay. Sloan and I thank you for considering and God Bless.

I hit post . . . not thirty seconds later I started getting notifications from Plumfund from family and friends. Then my Venmo account started pinging. $200.00, $50.00,

$500.00, $10.00, $25.00, $1,000.00 . . . it kept on coming. I couldn't respond fast enough either by calling or texting, and I definitely was not coherent.

Let me tell you, it is so much harder to receive than to give. It causes you to feel extreme humility. Over the next few weeks, we received over fifteen thousand dollars in Plumfund donations and numerous checks given privately from our loving family and friends. My cousin and her husband in Northern Indiana each year give a check to a family in need instead of sending a boatload of Christmas cards. We were THAT family this year. Talk about humbling . . .

The heart test comes back, and his injection fraction rate is normal! Praise God! We send the test results to Evoke and Blue Ridge. We wait for their response and they both say they'd love to have him! Carson makes phone calls one more time to each of the admissions counselors to ask more questions. Carson has really connected with Jon at Blue Ridge. Jon tells Carson that he has been in recovery for years and he encourages Carson that he too can have lifelong success in recovery. Carson picks Blue Ridge.

13.

And she loved a [not so] little boy very, very much, even more than she loved herself.

~Shel Silverstein, *The Giving Tree*

I have read stories of mothers who have lost their sons to drug overdose. There is a mom in Indiana who lost both of her boys on the same date, in the same house, to a fentanyl laced drug. I can't even imagine . . . however, maybe I can. I have seen my child gray and gasping for breaths, not sure if he was going to live.

November 19, at 6:00 p.m., we pick Carson up from Fairbanks. My parents meet us to give him hugs and say goodbye. We are not sure when they'll see him again. They are in their eighties.

We travel four-and-a-half hours to London, Kentucky, and get a hotel room. We are nervous and on edge. What keeps Carson from saying "Fuck this," and bolting? He wants to go out and have one more cigarette. Sloan goes with him. Carson is agreeable.

We wake early to get on the road, since Blue Ridge is expecting us by noon. Halfway to northern Georgia, we stop for a bathroom break at a McDonald's. As I walk in and head toward the bathroom, I notice a young man, maybe a year older than Carson. I notice that he looks rough, like he's homeless. He makes eye contact and my momma radar goes off. He is a drug addict. I know he was wondering if he could approach me for money. It's so sad to live in this realm when most would not even be observant enough to know what or who they are seeing. I come out of the bathroom and the young man is gone. I walk back to the car and see Sloan leaning against the car and see he is watching Carson smoke a cigarette with the young man. Sloan is also aware that this could be a potential risk. Drug addiction is sneaky. Carson gets back in the car and I can't help but ask. "Carson, did that guy give you anything?" He says no, shows me his pockets, opens his mouth, lifts his tongue. "He just wanted to bum a cigarette." I'm not relieved. I just want to get to Blue Ridge.

Ten minutes from Blue Ridge, Carson says he wants to have his last cigarette. We pull over at yet another McDonald's. I am pushing him to hurry, because we are late due to traffic through the mountains.

Finally, we arrive, and are greeted by the staff, who quickly tell us we only have five minutes to say goodbye. Carson takes nothing with him except the clothes on his back. They provide everything for living in the wilderness, underwear, socks, shoes . . . everything. Carson turns to hug me, and I begin to cry.

"Carson, God has a plan for you, and He loves you even more than I do."

He tells me he'll be OK and not to worry. He hugs Sloan. He, too, has tears. I have never seen Sloan cry as much in the twenty-five years we have been together as he has over Carson. An older couple come out to get him. We watch him walk down the hall before we leave. He is going to get outfitted and have a physical, and then they will take him to the young adult group called Emerald Arrow, somewhere in the Blue Ridge Mountains.

It is one in the afternoon and we decide to stay overnight instead of driving eight hours back home. We need to decompress. We find a cottage hotel to stay at in Clayton, Georgia. It's off-season, so the town, usually bustling with tourists who want to hike the many trails or start the Appalachian Trail, is vacant. We mindlessly go for a burger and visit a local market. We quietly watch the Georgia news. Sloan looks at trail maps, trying to figure out where they took Carson. I go to Facebook to post an update:

Sloan and I dropped Carson off at Blue Ridge Wilderness Therapy in Georgia today! I sobbed…. we will miss him….. won't get to see him for 5-6 weeks and he may never move back to Indy….that's OK….this is his chance to be born again! We want to thank you all for supporting us through prayers, gifts, and your generosity! We truly couldn't have done it without family and friends! It took a village to get this one boy where he is now! It reminds me of one of my favorite scriptures about the Shepherd who left his heard of 99 sheep to go and find the one, lonely, lost sheep. Thank you!

All the comments of compassion and solidarity started the tears flowing. I think years of tears came out. I couldn't stop. At times, I couldn't catch my breath. If I stopped, I'd start back up just trying to read the comments to Sloan. I think my resolve had turned into relief.

14.

Emerald Arrow: A Bold Path

*Reveal, Restore, Reclaim your
Deep-Rooted Belonging.*

Toward the end of the first week, Anne, Carson's therapist and the creator of this program, calls us to introduce herself and tell us how the process will go. We'll have check-ins with her weekly, and as needed with the family therapist, Lizzy. There is no contact with Carson, except through letters. This is a huge part of the therapy. Within a few weeks, Sloan and I will each submit our big letter, which explains the impact his use has had on us and the family. All letters go through Anne so she can coach us. They are meant to be truthful and raw.

At first Carson's letters are very upbeat and appreciative, kind of like, "Hey, Mom, camp is great." During one of our check-ins with Anne, we had a laugh over his surface-only representation of life in the wilderness. I said, "He is tenacious and masters just about anything he puts his mind to. Let's hope he can master sobriety." We agree that living in the wilderness is not his struggle.

The idea of living in the wilderness is to get back to basics. No distractions. Very simple living. No tents, just tarps. There are no more than twelve young adults at one time, coed. There are three to four field staff that live with them 24/7 and rotate into camp every six to eight days. Nurses come in every week for well-checks. Anne is with them two or more times a week but does not live with them. The field staff are trained to initiate and engage in the dynamics of the group and to build relationships individually. The students have, week to week, levels of homework called pathways. They are encouraged to journal, to talk openly. It truly is twenty-four-hour therapy, whether they know it or not. The kids hike from camp to camp every few days. There are foot checks to make sure they aren't getting "trench foot." One of the biggest things the students do is to master bow drilling, a way to make fire. It is incredibly hard and time-consuming. The process causes them to fail and succeed in a contained environment. The whole wilderness camp experience is various lessons in self and group reliance. They learn how to be honest, humble, and what it means to have integrity. Each student is there for different reasons. Not all are addicts, but most abuse substances due to self-medicating. Carson is the only one at the time dealing with addiction.

Carson is a total "too cool for school" kid. Come to find out, it's his defense mechanism, kind of a shield. Underneath, he struggles with social anxiety. He is quickly called out for his eye-rolling and general attitude. He starts to learn what it means to be authentic and transparent. It's hard for him because his way has become a habit, a way of navigating high school. During our second check-in with Anne, she informs us that there was an incident with another student. My heart sank; my stomach was in knots. "What happened?" I ask.

"It seems another student has a crush on Carson."

"Oh, really . . . ?" I'm like, "Oh, thank God!" We can work with this, I think.

She says this rarely happens, which she explains she is thankful for because it would be a pain in her ass. She then says, it's a young man.

I say, "OK, and???"

She chatted with the young man and then they chatted with Carson. She explains the whole process of communicating and reflecting. It's all part of the therapy, learning how to communicate. Carson reflected that he heard the young man, and "It was cool, he just doesn't play that way." They ended up being best buds in camp. Well, thank God we did something right!

We get our first set of pictures from the wilderness. It's Thanksgiving. The kids had a pilgrim's feast. Turkeys on the spit, homemade casseroles and pies. Carson is smiling. His cheeks are getting fuller. He is starting to look like himself again.

A couple weeks later it's time for Sloan and me to send our impact letters:

Dear Carson,

I'm going to start this letter saying that the words to follow are truthful, factual and are my honest emotions. Truth can be brutal. No other way to say it and so it can't be sugar coated.

The scariest thing that has ever happened to me is seeing you, my child, laying in the chair barely breathing with vomit coming out of your mouth. The most horrible sound I have ever heard was your dad's blood curdling scream when he realized you were not just a sleep in the chair. The next few minutes felt like hours. I ran downstairs to find you gasping…. I ran back upstairs to find the Narcan that I bought a year prior because I feared this would happen. As I called 911, I tried to figure out how to use the Narcan…. I failed…. it was an old type and because I was so distraught, I could not figure it out. Thank God the EMT's came quick…They administered 1 dose of nasal mist then started an IV of Narcan and rushed you off to the hospital. I took pictures of you in your comatose state and everyone working on you…trying to revive you. I had to…I needed you to see how your life was ending. I called Grandpa and Auntie Mern right after the ambulance left and they couldn't understand me because I was sobbing trying to say, "HE OVERDOSED!"

Let's go back in time, when you decided to take your experimentation to another level. You were 16 and you and some friends were going to try Xan bars. You took them all. You were high for 48 hours plus. During that time, you tried to jump out of a car, a window, a second story window. You tried to leave at night and your dad and Jackson had to restrain you. You punched, kicked and bit them both. During that first incident, I called 911 5 times before we could get you into Fairbanks to detox. This, I thought was the scariest time in our lives. You were in IOP and we let you have friends over and you got drunk and sick on some high alcohol content drink. We should have known then that you were heading down a slippery slope.

As I walk around the house, I feel your absence. I'm also reminded of your substance abuse by the holes in the wall where you ripped a picture off the wall, by the dent in the refrigerator and chips in the cabinet where you threw a chair at Jackson. I remember the lamp cord you cut and the knife mark above the door. These are some of the burdens of your addiction. There are lost days of work, money spent on lawyer and court costs and the cost of treatments. The worry is unbearable, my fear debilitating…. At first, I worried where you were going, who you were with. Later, I started to worry if you were going to be high at another family function. Now, I fear your death. I can remember telling you as we were going to your elementary friend's funeral, that this is a parent's worst nightmare and I begged you to stop. I know you have struggled with motivation to be sober. Why was his and Joey's deaths not enough motivation? You might not be able to answer this, yet. I hope you can figure it out while in the wilderness.

I miss you so much, but I have such anxiety about you coming home to live.

All the above is past memories. I am trying to forget the images of you at death's door. I am trying to not have worry, fear or anxiety. I have hope and faith in God that He has a plan for you…a purpose. God has given humans free will, but He always gives a road back to Him no matter how many times we step off the path. I'm actually excited to see where this journey takes you. I forgive you. I have learned over the years that forgiving someone does not condone the actions of that person, it just means that to forgive is to let it go and to move on. I'm logical in my thinking…. I know you didn't think you'd ever become addicted when you started experimenting. [That pleasure center in your brain was turned on and unfortunately you have all the risk factors.] In adolescence, we always think "it" won't ever happen to me. In adolescence we are riskier, always looking for a thrill, stretching the boundaries, pushing the limits. I love you; Carson and I'll always be in your corner. And, I'll always support your recovery.

XOXO Mom

Carson,

We saw some pictures from last week and it looks like you are doing better. Did you ever think two years ago that you would be spending part of your senior year in the Blue

Ridge mountains?? I did not see it coming, but I think God has given you a second chance and it's up to you to make the most of things.

I'm not exactly sure when you started using drugs, but I can tell you without a doubt that it turned your life upside down. You went from a smart, confident, likable, young man to a selfish mean-spirited teen only concerned about his next high. Everyday life around our home was so uncomfortable when you were using. Your mom and I had to hide all kinds of things around the house because you would either take it or consume it without a care.

There are too many examples of your drug induced selfish ways to tell, but I wanted to remind you of a few instances that really hurt our family. In the early stages of your addiction, you would come to family events high. We spent Thanksgiving and Christmas trying to explain to family members why you lost so much weight and why you were slurring your words. Your grandma would ask what was wrong with Carson? We knew you had taken something; we just didn't know what? When we would confront you about it, the denial and shouting match would start.

I really felt like your addiction started at the beginning of your sophomore year when you missed the first several weeks of school because you went on a Xanax bar bender. You became a completely different person. Totally combative and mean. We couldn't let you go to school like that and I had to call your football coach and explain why his star mental attitude winner wouldn't be playing football that season. We convinced you to go into recovery at Fairbanks hospital where you learned about addiction, but you refused to admit that you were an addict.

Coming out of Fairbanks, you understood the problems of addiction but refused to accept that you carry the burden of being an addict. You seemed to blame your mom and I for forcing you into recovery when in your mind you were fine and just like every other teenager. I'm sorry to tell you that you are not like others when it comes to consuming alcohol or drugs. Unfortunately, one usage leads to 10 which leads to 20 which leads to a self- induced disaster.

Now, before you feel sorry for yourself-DON'T. Many people including your uncles have experienced the exact same behaviors and over time learned how to overcome them. They will tell you that it is never easy, but you have the strength within you to recover and succeed.

I felt like once you were done with your first round of recovery, you slowly got back into your drug usage. Marijuana and alcohol would lead to stronger drugs to abuse. In December of 2018, I remember when you went on another Xanax bender. You lost tons of weight and started verbally abusing everyone who cared about you and questioned your behavior. I had to take your car away for your own safety. One day, you called me from Walgreens and said someone had stolen your car, when in fact you were so out of it that you didn't remember or realize we had a fight and I had taken your keys. I picked you up and brought you home and cried. My son was destroying his life and our family. The next day, we had to cancel a family gathering with your grandparents because you were high on Xanax. We felt helpless and were waiting for the next disaster to happen.

The spring of 2019 led to more destructive behavior. Once again, you went on a bender and missed weeks of school. I remember you showed up to your sectional baseball game high from the night before and you were so out of it your coach had to pull you from the game. I was so mad at you because you let your team down and you might have won the game had you been in your right mind. A week later, I physically tried to remove a bag of pills from your shorts and you hit and head butted me. We were done with your abuse and your mom called 911. To our surprise, you chose to go to jail rather than going back into recovery at Fairbanks. You spent 3 long days in jail, and we thought this was your rock bottom. In order to avoid probation and a record, you decided to go through recovery again at Fairbanks.

Your mind set was a little different this time at Fairbanks. I think you did admit that you are an addict which was a first. You said you thought you could handle taking drugs casually when in fact you can't. You were saying all the right things throughout this round of recovery. Even your advice to other addicts going through recovery gave us hope that you were buying into your sobriety. We didn't know that you had bought a Xanax and were holding on to it until you got out of recovery. Your first day out of recovery, you took that pill and went to school high. We got word from some of your friends at school that you weren't acting right, and we were devastated. We felt so helpless and wondered if our loving son would ever come back?

From here, you know how the story ends. Your drug use goes from casual to acute. The lying, the verbal and physical abuse continue and lead to a devastating boiling point. I'll never forget October 18th. I wake up for work at 4am and come downstairs to find you in our living room unresponsive and gasping for air. You were aspirating. I screamed to your mom and she ran down and called 911. I stuck my fingers in your mouth to make sure you continued to breathe while we were waiting for the ambulance. When the paramedics arrived, they quickly took over, administered Narcan for a heroin overdose and rushed you off to the hospital. We had no idea if you would survive or be brain dead. We said a quick prayer and rushed off to the hospital.

The trauma doctor said that your heart and lungs were severely damaged, and it would take hours/days to truly know the extent. I'm not the most spiritual person but I prayed for your recovery and lifted you up to God. I wanted my son back. I prayed for strength within you to recover and succeed. I do realize that I can help give you the tools to recover, but that your recovery is ultimately up to YOU.

As time has passed, I have experienced so many emotions. At first, I felt sad and didn't want to talk with anyone. Then I felt anger and was mad about the hurt you have caused this family. When you went to Blue Ridge, I finally felt peace that you were taking responsibility for yourself and your recovery. Your mom has helped me to let go of this anger and lift it up to God.

The glorious thing about your story is that it has NOT ended, and that God has given you a second chance. I look at your recent pictures of you smiling and I can envision so many bright and positive things in your future without drugs. I can't forget the hurt that your actions have caused this family, but I have forgiven you because I realized the power these drugs had over you. Because of Fairbanks and Blue Ridge Therapy programs, you now have the knowledge and strength to resist your urges. It's time to grow up and take responsibility for your actions and I know you can do it. Please know that I love you and I believe in you. I can't wait to see you in the near future so we can talk and continue our healing. Stay strong son. I LOVE YOU, Dad

Anne tells us that when she brought our letters to Carson, he became nervous. The process is for him to read our letters in front of the group first thing. He does not get to preview. This was the first time she saw him shed tears.

The group asked questions and gave feedback. The other students could feel the pain we expressed but also told him that they saw hope. The other students were taken aback by the extent of his drug use. I guess he hadn't truly bared his soul yet.

The next letter we receive from Carson is his response to our impact letters.

Dear Mom,

I would like to start off this letter by saying how truly thankful and grateful I am for this impact letter in which you have written. I'm grateful that I have such a courageous mom who is able to share with me the brutal truth and emotions that come out of result of my actions.

From your letter I hear that my actions and decisions has led to the most fearful moment in your life, which was when you and dad found me unconscious and gasping for air on October 18th of 2019. You felt as if this traumatic experience went on for much longer than it actually was. I hear that you might have some regret and guilt for not being able to figure out the Narcan. You had taken pictures of me in this state for the reason that if I would survive, you wanted me to see firsthand where my addiction had brought me. This situation had you so fearful that you would never see me again. This thought left you sobbing and unable to communicate. Reading this made me feel shame because of who I have become, and the guilt for putting you two through that.

You brought up the time when I had taken 8 Xanax. This was the first time you had seen my experimentation escalate. The prolonged effects the Xanax had on me influenced you to be anxious and fearful. You felt completely powerless in this moment. I hear the actions I made during this state such as physically fighting Dad and Jackson, and trying to run away, made you feel as if the only way you could help was to call the police on your own son. The emotions that came up for me when I read this was a lot of guilt and the wish to take it all back.

I hear that you feel my absence at home but are mainly reminded of my substance abuse by the physical damage that I have caused to the house over the years. I also hear the financial loss in which was a result of my using such as court costs, treatment costs, and medical bills. You've always worried about me, but over the years and as my addiction got worse the aspects in which you would worry also started to change. You fear my death. You have confusion on why Joey and my elementary friend's death were never enough motivation for me to end my using. This left me feeling selfish because I made the choice to continue using when you begged me to stop.

I hear that you miss me, and you don't miss the using Carson. You feel as if we can't live together again and that you have a lot of fear regarding my future. You hate feeling this way, and I hear I've caused you so much hurt and pain. You feel that distance is necessary for my survival. I've manipulated and lied to you so much that it's hard for you to differentiate rewards from enabling. I hear that detaching from your child does not come easy to you. This part of the letter brought up overall sadness and emotional pain.

I hear you have trouble visualizing me living a clean and purposeful life. You believe that I have gifts that can promise this type of life. You see me as a leader, although I never want to take on that challenge. You guess it's because of my lack of confidence. You have longing for old Carson and cherish the times we've spent together in the past. Such as family vacations. It's hard, but you are trying to forget the images of me at death's door. You're hopeful that God has a plan for me, and you are excited to see where this journey leads. I hear you forgive me and that does not condone my actions. This made me feel so hopeful for the future, and it shed a lot of light where it previously lacked.

Your support means everything to me and without it I feel as if it'd be impossible. This letter meant a lot to me and it was difficult to read at moments. It made me feel a lot of emotions I haven't been able to feel in a long time. I love and respect you so much and I understand completely where you are coming from.

Love, Carson (Bubba Wubba)

Dear Dad,

I know that you have been busy during this time of year, and I want you to know how appreciative I am for you taking the time to speak your emotions. I know it's been hard to communicate in the past, and I partially feel that you held back your opinions and emotions because you were scared of how I'd react. I don't blame you for this. When I am using, I am mean and an unthoughtful person who is closeminded. I want you to know that you don't have to worry about that this time around, you are entitled to have these emotions. I'm all ears.

I hear that you believe that I was smart, confident, likeable man before I started using. You feel that drugs turned my life upside down and turned me into a selfish, mean-spirited teen who only worried and cared about my next high. I hear that life at home was uncomfortable for you and the family when I was using. You feel that there are too many examples of my drug induced selfish ways to tell. You mentioned how I would constantly be showing up to family events high. I hear you spent Thanksgiving and Christmas trying to explain to family members why I was acting the way I was. This would follow with a denial and shouting match on my end. Reading this brought up emotions of guilt and shame when you described your perception of me while using.

You feel that my addiction really took off at the beginning of my sophomore year, when I missed the first couple of weeks because of my Xanax bender. I hear that Xanax changed me for the worse. I became mean. I hear you had to call and personally tell my football coach why I wouldn't be playing that season. You and mom convinced me to get treatment at Fairbanks. I hear that you witnessed me refusing that I was not an addict at that time.

I hear that you feel that I blamed you and mom for forcing me into recovery, because I still felt I was fine, and I wasn't an addict. You're sorry, but you tell me that I'm not like every other teenager when it comes to using. You tell me not to feel sorry for myself, and that a lot of people go through what I'm going through. I hear that you believe I have the strength to recover from this disease. Reading this makes me feel hopeful knowing that I'm not alone in this struggle.

I hear that once I got out of rehab the first time, you believe that my drug usage slowly got more severe. In December of 2018 that you remember when I went on another Xanax bender. This resulted in me losing a ton of weight. I hear that I was verbally abusing everyone who cared about me. I hear you had taken away my car for my own safety. I was so out of it when I walked to Walgreens, I thought someone had stolen my car. I was so high I forgot you had taken my keys. This made you cry, you felt that your son was destroying his life and our family. The next day you had to cancel family gathering because I was too high to function. I hear that this left you feeling so helpless.

I hear that in the Spring of 2019 you remember me on another bender, where I yet again missed weeks of school. I hear that you were so mad when I played my sectional baseball game high. You feel that I let down my team. I hear that a week later you physically tried to remove pills from my possession, and I hit, and head butted you. The police were called, and you were surprised that I chose jail over another round of rehab. After my time spent in jail, I decided to go through recovery treatment again. This made me feel shame and regret.

I hear you witnessed me fake my way through recovery yet again, and I used the first day out of rehab. This left you feeling powerless and wondering if your loving son would ever come back. I hear that from here my drug use went from casual to acute. You will never forget October 18th when you found me unresponsive and gasping for air. I hear you and mom called 911 and while waiting for the ambulance you stuck your fingers in my mouth to make sure I kept breathing. When the EMTs arrived they administered Narcan and rushed me to the hospital. You and mom said, and quick prayer then left for the hospital.

I hear the trauma doctor said that my heart and lungs were damaged and that the true extent was unknown. I hear that you prayed for recovery and put me in God's hands. I hear that you realize that my recovery is ultimately up to me and that there's not a lot you can do. This part of the letter made me feel guilty for putting you through such a traumatic situation.

I hear that as time passed, you have been overwhelmed with many emotions. At first you experienced sadness, then it was anger and you were mad about the hurt I have caused the family. I hear that you finally felt peace once I went off to Blue Ridge. You are grateful that I have a second chance at life, and I hear that you forgive me. This made me feel so loved and grateful to have you in my life. This letter brought up a lot of emotions for me, and I am grateful that you wrote it. I look forward to further communication and vulnerability with each other. I love you so much.

Love, Carson

15.

"Check-in"

A brief discussion about one's present emotional and cognitive state.

It's been five weeks since we dropped Carson off to live a nomadic life. We get to visit him for an afternoon and then attend a parent workshop for a couple days. It's January and instead of driving, we choose to fly, never quite sure what the mountain roads will be like in winter. We fly into Atlanta and drive to North Georgia. I am so excited and yet really nervous. All his letters indicate that "it" (wilderness therapy) is working. However, I know we have PTSD from living with the manipulation for so long that I worry he is just faking it till he can run. I pray a lot-- and my faith is strong, but I can't help waiting for another "shoe to drop."

We finally get to meet Anne in person the morning after we arrive. There is another couple visiting their son in the young adult group. After a short meeting with Anne explaining how the day will go, we get in our separate cars and follow her into the Blue Ridge Mountains on the North Carolina side. It takes us about thirty to forty minutes, and as we climb higher and higher, I think, if Carson or any other student tried to run, how would they ever find them?

We arrive and park on the forestry road near their camp. Since we are in a rental car, he can't tell which one is us. I round the bumper, and he full-on bolts toward me and gives me the biggest bear hug and lifts me off the ground, which is not an easy feat. We hug and hug and hug till finally Sloan says, "Hey, can I get some of that?!"

Carson shows us around camp: where they circle up around the fire, where he sleeps, where the staff sleep, where they go #2, how they protect their food from the bears, how they filter water from the stream. It's incredible how well-organized camp is. Everyone has chores along with their own care for their gear.

Anne asks the staff to call a circle for introductions. We stand around the fire while everyone takes turns introducing themselves. They tell us where they are from and a few things about themselves. Even we have a go. At the moment students make up is all guys and one trans girl. Since the students come into Blue Ridge at different times, the other students' parents have already visited or will at a later date.

After circling up, Carson takes us to an area he has set up just for us. He starts a fire with embers from the main fire. He says he'll show us bow drilling soon. We sit around the awesome fire he has made and eat gorp (trail mix) and visit. He is so chatty, filling us in on his New Year's hike, the other students, and the staff. Anne comes over for our family session. Carson has written out an "I feel" statement for each of us. He and Anne explain this is how they communicate. It is part of the checking-in process. Anyone can call a check-in at any time. It's meant to practice awareness and communication.

Carson starts to read me his "I feel" statement directed solely to me. He is nervous and keeps looking at Anne and saying, "It's not her fault." She encourages him to keep going. Carson says to me that he wishes I would have said "no" more. No to going places, but money, especially. Again, he says to me, "I am an addict. It's not your fault, I manipulated you." Anne encourages us to stay on the format.

Then it's my turn to reflect back to him. I say to him that I hear him and that I am not offended by him wishing that I'd said "no" more. I get it.

"Carson, let me tell you where I come from when it comes to parenting. My mom was always saying no. She wouldn't even wait to hear my entire statement before saying no. I knew that I wanted to be a 'yes' parent, within boundaries, of course. I believe in rewarding good behavior. So, when you would go to school, and to work, and to therapy and to a meeting, your dad and I would be OK with giving you a tenner to go to McDonalds."

Carson replies with, "Toward the end, Mom, I spent it on heroin."

"Carson, I have a feeling you were screaming in your head, 'SAY NO, SAVE ME!'"

He puts his head down and says again, "It's not your fault, you didn't make me an addict."

I cry. Don't we all just want our parents to save us?

Carson gives his "I feel" statement to Sloan. He tells Sloan that he has not felt connected to him for a long time. That even though Sloan was physically at every game, concert, event-- he felt a disconnect, a judgment. Sloan reflects what he hears Carson saying and explains that his father was an alcoholic and was not present, so he had no training in fatherhood. He was flying by the seat of his pants. Sloan admitted to Carson that over this past year, he was so distraught over Carson's use that he had no words. Maybe that was what Carson thought was judgment. The lack of conversation. But what do you say when you watch your son deteriorate before your eyes? Anne has Carson teach Sloan bow drilling by doing so tandemly. Even though sparks might not have flown, and no embers were made, I witnessed the rebirth of connection between Sloan and Carson.

It's time to go . . . we have been with Carson for four hours out of a four-day trip. I am amazed at how far he has come in five weeks. Though we are not sure how long he will be in the wilderness, we are confident this is where he needs to be. Now, it's time for some processing time for Sloan and me alongside other parents who are struggling to parent their teen or young adult. Our workshop starts with a "get to know you" dinner at one of the local bed and breakfasts.

The next morning, we arrive early to an incredible Southern breakfast. The family therapists, Kayla and Lizzy, have developed this workshop of education, reflection, processing, and practicing with a side of pampering to lift us parents up. They know we are just as broken as our children. We sit in a large circle. There are about ten couples, with even a set of stepparents who have come to learn how to support their stepchild. Not going to lie, we all look like deer in headlights. Even though each family's story is different, we all come from the same place of anguish. As I look around the room and think, "Toto, we aren't in Kansas anymore," I am reminded of a friend back home who had a psychiatrist explain simply the levels of teens.

Level one is your typical teen who experiments, explores, and pushes the boundaries. He or she is the teen that says, "OK, I'll TRY that" (sex, drugs, stealing, skipping school). Level two is the kid who says, "OK, yeah sure, I'll go BUY it." Level three is the young person who takes it all to the next level. They have done all the drugs, they have been promiscuous, they have jumped out of second-story windows to go party with friends or to meet their drug dealer, they might have even attempted suicide. These kids also have or will get another diagnosis outside of being your "typical teen." It could range from substance use disorder to depression, bi-polar, generalized anxiety, etc. Again, I look around the room and think, "Yep, we all have level three youth."

Kayla and Lizzy begin the workshop. They tell us the objectives for the next day and a half. We jump right in with our hopes and fears surrounding our youth. I hope to stop enabling. I hope to not be manipulated. I hope to not worry about either son's future. I hope we have enough money to pay for his continued care. I fear I'll fall into the same anxious patterns if he relapses. I fear I will go broke. I fear that I will collapse into depression if he doesn't succeed in sobriety. I fear that he will overdose again. We all take a moment to share amongst each other. Tears start to fall around the circle, not just from our own realizations but also from hearing and acknowledging the other parents' hopes and fears.

We learn and reflect on different communication patterns, de-escalation techniques, barriers to communication, wheel of emotions, the shame cycle, the drama triangle, and so forth. We have meals together and take a long walk.

Toward the end of the workshop, we break into small groups to practice the check-in process of communication that we did with our kid in the woods. I say, "I feel anxious and scared that this all won't work, and he'll give up and go back to using. My body reacts by breathing shallow and my heart palpitating. I choose to respond by praying and talking about my fears."

Another parent reflects back to me that he heard me and gives feedback. "I am a recovering addict," he says. "Like we say to ourselves, I say to you . . . think 'One day at a time.' Try not to think too far in the future because you can't predict it, so why torture yourself in the what-ifs . . ." He continues, "I suggest you and your husband go to Al-Anon Family Group meetings back home. Until then, remember these words from Al-Anon: I didn't cause it, I can't control it, and I can't cure it."

We meet for breakfast and a wrap up the last day. We hug our fellow parents and the therapists. We all agree to meet up on our closed Facebook page. I am exhausted, we all are. I feel more equipped to tackle or handle what comes my way in regard to Carson, and even our older son. We take off to head back to Atlanta to fly home. We decide to stop off at a McDonald's to have a quick bite.

Sloan goes to the restroom while I get our meals, and when he comes out, I am sitting at a table crying into my quarter pounder. "What's wrong, why are you crying?" he says to me.

"It's just so much . . . " I tell him.

He looks at me perplexed and just lets me cry as we eat together silently. I think he sees my tears as sadness while he just had an experience of hopefulness. I'm not sad, I am hopeful. My emotions come from exhaustion of keeping my shit together over these past few days. Maybe I should have let it all spill out . . . I don't know if I could have at the time. This is the time I decided to let it out . . . over a quarter pounder!

16.

"Too many times, I swallowed my pride,
I'm cracking a smile, I'm dying inside,
My demons are close, I'm trying to hide,
I'm poppin' a pill, I'm feeling alive...I'm
feeling alive..."

~ J Cole

The week after we get home from visiting Carson,
we receive a weekly letter.

Dear Mom and Dad,

I wanted to let you all know that seeing you last week and introducing you guys to the woods was so much fun and beneficial. For your informationI busted 2 fires the day after you left.

Carson had said he had lost his mojo in busting for a couple weeks.

I felt that all of our conversations were very meaningful, especially the one about communication, dad. I'm very excited for the future in regard to our relationship and being vulnerable with each other.

The weather here has been pretty awful. It's not been cold but it sure is raining a lot. Please tell Grandpa and Grandma that I love them, and I really enjoy their letters last week. Oh, and mom, please send an email to Alison saying that I am doing good, working hard and regularly thinking about the Fairbanks family and how much they've supported me.

Sorry for the short letter, I'm being rushed. I love you both and Jackson, too. Please wish him luck in his second semester. Love, Carson

This letter speaks volumes on the changes he is going through. Because of our PTSD, there is a small part of us that thinks, "Is he bullshitting his way through?"

Over the past few weeks, Anne had started a conversation with us about Carson having a psychological assessment done. We had started that process at home with the Psychiatric Center at our Children's Hospital after Carson had a panic attack. I don't doubt that there might be a dual diagnosis. When dealing with adolescence, especially today with technology at our fingertips 24/7, it just seems that anxiety and depression is a common theme, let alone any genetic component. We decide that knowledge is power, and on the advice of a dear friend who is a parenting expert, she says any nugget of insight into Carson's psychological functioning will help with his overall treatment. We already know that he started out his elementary years with an auditory processing disorder that my childhood best friend, the audiologist, spent an entire summer working with him on. There just might be more answers.

After filling out several forms and surveys, and Carson doing the same, along with speaking with the psychologist, the evaluation came back. The good news is no major psychosis was detected. He has average IQ and EQ. He has a severe substance abuse disorder . . . yep . . .along with social and generalized anxiety. His learning disability was detected. His processing speed is deficient. He claims it has always taken him longer to comprehend what he is learning. We have food for thought and now it's time to move on and forward.

It's the first of February and Carson's letter of accountability comes through the parent portal. He has been in the wilderness ten weeks-- and sober over 100 days. This is the longest he has gone without using since that fateful time at the beginning of his sophomore year.

Dear Mom and Dad,

In this letter I will be taking responsibility for the various actions in which I have been guilty of over the past couple of years. I will also be talking about how I was feeling and what was going on for me during those days. This is to give you guys more insight in to why I acted in these ways and what my thought process was. I have a feeling that you two already know a lot of what will be in this letter, but I hope that it brings some sort of peace and closure.

The first thing I am taking accountability for is my substance abuse. Through this action I was seeking love and belonging and trying to find and fulfill some type of freedom. Later on, in my addiction I was using drugs to fill a void in my life. I started smoking weed when I was 15. Jackson introduced me to it. I smoked all throughout high school and it caused me a bunch of trouble. The first time I got in trouble with the law was when my using buddies and I got caught smoking behind the old Applebee's. Xanax has been a really prevalent issue in the past three years of my life. My first trip to rehab was a result of a Xanax bender. During this I tried to run away. I physically assaulted my dad and brother, I tried to jump out of a moving car. Opiates became my preference in regard to drugs really quick. One of my childhood friends was my pill dealer during my junior year. Over the period of a couple months, I would purchase and take oxycodone 30mgs and 80mgs daily. This resulted in me going through withdrawals when his supply was gone. I hid this from you two. All throughout my experience at Shortridge, I was constantly buying and stealing my fellow students Adderall and ADHD meds. I used them to feel confident and smart. The time when I visited Purdue with you both and you suspected I was on something because of how talkative I was...you were correct. I had taken a 30mg extended-release Adderall to strengthen my focus during the college interview. On Thanksgiving 2018, I embarrassed myself and my family because I decided to take Xanax and drink. This extremely affected me and my family's relationship. I had taken pills on Thanksgiving because I was so nervous and anxious about being around so many family members. I have taken barbiturates one time, but this experience ended horribly for me. I was high and thinking so irrationally, I physically attacked you, dad, when you were trying to take the pills away from me. This resulted in the cops being called and me choosing to go to jail. In this moment my thinking was skewed, and I was feeling attacked and trapped. I started using heroin in September of 2019. I was using about once every other day. I was first tricked into taking it by a dealer who just wanted my money. My use of heroin resulted in me almost losing my life. The majority of my off days from school were spent searching for heroin and I am guilty of going to my level up meeting with Sarah high on heroin. Drugs made me feel confident and accepted by others, but more importantly I accepted myself. The impulse I had for taking mind altering substances made me feel in control. I was fully making my own decisions. Being high all the time, helped me to not feel emotions I didn't want to feel. Deep down I was lonely, fearful, anxious, and surrounded by a bunch of shame. Over the years, my using has caused me and the people around me a lot of pain. I've missed a lot of school, faced legal troubles and went to jail. I have negatively affected relationships with both my family and friends. I almost lost my life to the depths of my addiction. Throughout my use, I was so blind to the fact that all my actions were going against what really mattered to me, respect, honesty, family, self-care, faith, and confidence. I thought I was reaching for fun and adventure, but I wasn't thinking straight. Moving forward I intend to maintain my sobriety and reach a purposeful and happy life without the use of drugs by changing my environment, meeting new people and finding new and healthy hobbies.

Manipulation is another in which I want to take accountability for. I manipulated a lot of people including you guys for the result to get what I wanted. I was seeking power over a situation. Some examples of me manipulating are me telling you, mom, on one of my days off from school that I was going to Qdoba, drop a sweatshirt off at a friend's and to get my schedule at work. The fact that I used "chores" to convince you to let me take the car was manipulation of your permission. I wanted to buy myself as much time as possible to be able to take my heroin dealer to a pickup. I manipulated both of you into thinking I was sober by continuing to show up to meetings, therapy with Sarah and faking drug screens at the Dual Diagnosis program by using fake pee. I was wanting to make you two not suspicious so I could continue to use. Successfully manipulating someone made me feel as if I had control over them.

During the act of manipulation, I was probably feeling the emotions of sadness and anxiety. I would feel sad because I knew what I was doing was wrong and the thought that the person would catch on gave me intense anxiety. Because of my manipulation, my family began to lose a lot of trust in me and would constantly second guess my motives.

Through this, I was missing out on deep and loving connections with the people around me. My family was slowly becoming unable to recognize me emotionally. In the future, I know it will be hard to change my old habits, but I challenge all my friends and family to call me out when they notice my manipulating behavior.

Over the past couple of years, and in the midst of my addiction, I had begun skipping school pretty frequently. It came to a point where going to school sober was emotionally and physically impossible. By skipping school, I was trying to seek freedom and to have some fun to avoid my overwhelming boredom. School for me has always been a super anxious and stressful experience. I found myself always comparing myself to others whether that be on appearance or intelligence. I always felt that I needed to meet the same grades and accomplishments as my friends and other people I hung out with. This put a lot of pressure on me. Early on in high school I noticed that assignments and reading took me twice as long as my classmates. This made me frustrated and upset with myself. Because of this, it made me want to avoid and procrastinate on assignments. The time when we had a meeting with Mr. O'Day and Mr. Pactor about my attendance, I lied to you all saying I was sick, so I sat in my car all day. Really what happened was I went to smoke weed with some friends. I am guilty of skipping school to give plasma for money. I received $80.00 and used that money to buy Xanax. I felt shame for this. There was a time in my junior year after my 18th birthday where I told you, mom, I was going to go vote and that'd

I would be missing first period. I never ended up voting and skipped for the rest of the day to smoke weed. Most of the time I would either leave, or not show up to do drugs. Skipping school made me anxious and stressed. I was always fearful of getting caught. Doing drugs took my mind off of all the worrying. There are multiple times in which the school had called you because I didn't show up. You took away my car for a period of time. Skipping school caused me to miss out on something I truly cared about, which is education. Although I would not show up to school, I would always feel guilty. Though I have graduated, moving forward I plan to allow my parents to track me using Find a Friend so they can hold me accountable.

Stealing is a habit that I became way too comfortable with. I stole to feel a sense of power and control over the things I wanted. Stealing became an impulse action for me, but it never got easier. Stealing would instantly make me feel regretful and guilty and my addiction was the main influence for these actions. I am guilty of stealing money from both of you. Either from your purse or wallet or lying about not having any change when you gave me money for gas or food. Yes, most of the money went to drugs to feed my addiction. Something in which I am really ashamed of is stealing

$80.00 in quarters from Grandma Clara's quarter collection. This money was spent on heroin. The time when dad had his back surgery and his prescription narcos were replaced with similar looking Tylenol, you assumed it was me. Dad and you confronted me on it. I continued to deny and lie that I had nothing to do with it. You were both correct, I took the pills. At first when I found where you were hiding them, I only planned to take four. This was not the case, and I kept going back for more. Over a period of a week, I had taken all of them. I knew I was going to get caught, but my addiction pushed me to take them anyways. I figured my best bet was to fill the script with Tylenol. Back when Mom would hide her work funds in the desk in her studio, I would every once in a while sneak in and take a $10 or a $20. Mom caught on and started hiding her money elsewhere. The time when I was watching the neighbor's dog, I found the boy's hydrocodone syrup when rummaging through their medicine cabinet. I drank about 8 oz. of it. Dad almost caught me taking it, when he came to check on me. I filled the rest of the bottle with water to not get caught. Because of my stealing and sneakiness, you two became suspicious and started hiding everything valuable. Money, keys, prescriptions, etc. I was never grateful of how much you two supported and provided for me and these are prime example of this. My addict tendencies always made me need more than I had. For the future I intend to be as self-sufficient as possible, and to be more giving to others.

I've been disrespectful over the past couple of years. Drugs made me become a mean-spirited person with a short temper, I only cared about myself. A lot of the time my disrespect came from a place of defensiveness when I knew I was in the wrong. During my first Xanax bender, which landed me in rehab, I acted brutally mean, abusive, and disrespectful. I called you, mom, a bitch. I threw a chair at Jackson and I was verbally abusive to everyone who was trying to help me. This circumstance made me feel trapped and personally attacked. All the attention was on me and I just wanted to be left alone. Another example of my disrespectfulness was me sneaking out of the house at night, even after all the times you guys asked me to stay in. One time was the first time I snuck out. It was freshman year; I was 15 and didn't have my license yet. I jumped out of the second story window and took the Camry out for a joy ride. I met a couple of girls and bought and smoked weed. I drove your car under the influence of drugs. Another instance of my disrespect was me drinking with a bunch of friends at the house when I was in rehab the first time. You set boundaries and said it was a sober household and I proceeded to cross those boundaries. This resulted in me getting sick. I was trying to have what I thought was fun and feel as if I wasn't missing out because I was in IOP. I thought that if I just drank, I could avoid it showing up on a drug test. Putting people down and saying hurtful things made me feel powerful as if I had won an argument. Once I began being disrespectful, my pride wouldn't let me stop. This made me feel instant regret. The disrespectfulness I displayed earned me groundings such as my car and phone being taken away. During those times of dis-respect, I was close- minded, not supportive and super defiant. In the future my intentions are to be more open-minded to others and to take space for myself when my anger start to escalate.

Lying has been another huge bad habit of mine. By lying I was trying to seek freedom and control. I am guilty of lying to get out of trouble. I would often lie about where I was and who I was with, to get more freedom and leniency from you both. I'd lie to avoid suspicion. My addiction has influenced me to take on a very unhealthy habit of lying and it became impulsive. In September of 2019, you guys called me home to talk. You said someone had informed you that I was looking for heroin. You gave me a chance to be honest and I continually lied and got defensive. The truth is, I was on heroin then. I was so ashamed to admit it to you guys. Right before Thanksgiving 2018, mom you took me to the doctor to find out why I had lost so much weight. They tested my blood and it came back positive for opiates. I told you that a friend had given me a 5mg of hydro for a migraine. The truth is I took an 80mg of oxy the day before the doctor's appointment. I was so caught up in a long series of lies I knew of nothing else to do but to continue lying. I would get instantly anxious, worrying I'd get caught in a lie but when it'd work out, I'd have a feeling of confidence. Because of my lying, I lost a lot of trust with you both. My addiction got a lot worse because I would lie to myself and to my friends. I had no gratitude for what you two have done for me. Moving forward I plan to reach out for help and support before I act on a thought I will regret.

Here at Blue Ridge, I've made progress in creating healthy habits. I've been practicing to re-wire my brain by communicating my urges and cravings before I act on them. I have done this by learning to use "I feel statements" and by "checking in" with the group. I've been working on gaining confidence in my opinions and in stating my feelings. This is a long and positive process. I have been using the "feedback" format to voice my opinions and thoughts in a way that I will feel heard. The relationships I have built here are on a deep level of connection and are super meaningful to me. I've met so many supportive and caring people who are sober and engage in healthy activities. They, too, are trying to change for the better. I have learned self-awareness of my mind and body, and I am learning how to identify when I'm avoiding and distracting myself. Since being here, I've noticed that I have used things here besides drugs to use. Bow drilling has been a really positive yet delayed sense of gratification for me in the woods. I've used food as a way to seek satisfaction and I daydream about fantasies to take myself out of the present and to avoid stressful situations. I have become aware of my addictive tendencies and my strive to always want or need more. This has taught me to be content with myself and my accomplishments and to enjoy them.

Thank you for reading my letter of accountability. It feels very empowering and renewing to take responsibility and to come completely clean of all my actions and to have healthy plans for moving forward. I hope you two gain something from this and I can't wait to hear your responses. For the future, I hope to maintain a close, healthy, and vulnerable relationship with you both and Jackson. I hope I can show you guys all I've learned by taking our own camping trip. We can incorporate the therapeutic skills I have learned into the family dynamic. As a result, to all this, I have faith that over time I will continue to build trust.

Love, Carson

I needed to read his letter several times to grasp all that I was reading. As I read my mouth would just hang open and I would think . . . "I never knew" or "Why didn't he say something?" As a parent, a mother more so, you *know* your child! Obviously, I did not. He internalized so much and because he was not a chatty kid like his brother he definitely did not speak up. He seemed so confident . . . he could do anything from climbing a tree to playing football and baseball to skateboarding like Tony Hawk. Why couldn't he see what we saw? When did it all change for him? Middle school? High school? Could we have intervened if we had known how he was feeling, or how he viewed himself? I guess it proves that you can be so involved, so supportive, in your kid's life and yet still be clueless.

17.

Treatment should address the needs of the whole person, rather than just focusing on their drug use.

National Institute on Drug Abuse

In most cases, kids/young adults don't go home from the wilderness. They move on to a residential treatment center, behavioral boarding school or sober-living programs. Again, not near home. Anne encourages us to hire a therapeutic consultant and gives us names. We choose Kim from One Oak Consulting out of Chicago. She has worked extensively in the addictions world. She has vetted many programs around the country. After talking with us and having conversations with Carson, trying to get a feel of what he wants in a program, she gives Sloan and me six programs to contact: two in southern California, one in Florida, one in North Carolina, one in Utah, and one in Maine. We have learned that most addicts will stick around where their residential treatment or sober living program is. Usually, there are large sober communities in the areas where there are recovery programs. Honestly, we don't want him to ever come back to Indiana to live. In recovery, you have to change the people, places, and things that got you sick. I'm sure years from now when he is mature and has been living a sober life for years, he could try, but for now, we need to assume that he will stay and live where he finally chooses his program.

Sloan and I quickly rule out the California and Florida programs. Call it intuition, but I couldn't see Carson living after the program is finished in those areas. Certainly not in a healthy, sober way. We call and talk to the programs in Utah, Maine, and North Carolina. We have worked out financials with all three and feel comfortable with Carson choosing any of these programs. We tell Kim and Anne and they set up phone calls from the field. Carson now has a chance to gain control of his future. He will have buy-in. At the last minute, Kim pulls the Maine program. She and Anne feel that that program might have too much freedom out of the gate. Carson calls Balance House in Utah and Recovery House in North Carolina. We will soon see what he chooses. My gut tells me he should pick the mountains as opposed to the beach environment. Both programs seem suited for him, but environment is key to ultimate change. After a week or so, Carson writes to tell us he has picked Utah. Oh, thank God!

It's getting close to graduation from the wilderness. We have our weekly call with Anne. She begins the update on Carson with "So . . . " Usually in our family when someone starts a conversation with "So," it is followed by bad news. My heart starts to race, my stomach tightens, my throat constricts. I think Carson has run away . . . he stole meds from the medicine box. I can't help but think the worst. Anne continues on to say that Carson and another student have had an altercation. What started as Carson roughhousing with this student turned into where the student felt uncomfortable. The rules of the wilderness are there is no physical touch unless initiated by the group as a whole, like a group hug. Anne explains that when she confronted Carson, she was quite stern. It made him show really raw emotion that he hadn't really shown. He thought that he had ruined months of progress and he was convinced Anne was going to kick him out of the program. Anne felt the timing was perfect to send Carson on his "walkabout."

Dear Mom and Dad,

You probably have already heard, but I am currently on a solo away from the group. Anne assigned this to me because I was roughhousing with another student. When I first heard this, I was super sad and frustrated. I didn't want to end my time here on a bad note. I saw it as a negative punishment.

Since then, my perception of this situation has changed drastically. I'm excited about my solo/walkabout. I see it as a wonderful opportunity and a growth edge. God has a plan for everything, I couldn't have done anything different. This is his path for me. I'm aware I have made mistakes and

I will most likely continue to make mistakes down the road. The important thing is how I choose to learn from them. It's a powerful thing to sit in silence and isolation, so much can arrive from it. Feelings, thoughts, intentions and awareness.

I hope you two can see it as a blessing like I have. At first, I thought of it as two steps back, but it is not. It's an opportunity that allows me to leap forward.

Prior to my solo, I had been working on stepping up in a leadership and trying to keep the group and myself accountable of the boundaries. Obviously, I had a little hiccup to the boundaries part. I am working on that.

I love you two very much and can't wait to give you hugs when I see you next.

Love, Carsey Warsey

A week later, we receive another letter from Carson.

Dear Mom and Dad,

I am very happy and proud to tell you that my walkabout was extremely life-changing and influential. Living in solitude with much time for introspection was so beneficial for me. I learned a lot about integrity, which is doing the right thing even when no one is looking. For me in the past, when no one was looking it was go time, whether that be snorting a line or sneaking a $20 from your wallets. I realize that for the future, integrity is something I really need to work on. It's the decider of life and death. If I'm in a situation where drugs are being offered, I have to have integrity to say no. I'm an adult now, and I want to be surrounded by supportive people. If I can't make integrous decisions and choices, sooner or later I'm going to die. That's just the harsh truth.

I came to the awareness that I live my life worrying too much about what other people want and think of me. I just need to show up how I want to show up and everyone else's reaction to me is out of my control. I need to be comfortable with just being me. In school, it was never "cool" to follow boundaries and rules. I always hung with people who broke or bent the rules. This transferred over to my experience at Blue Ridge and how I've had trouble following the rules. This was usually to get a reaction or impress someone…A girl.

Since I have reintegrated back into the group, I have been extremely happy and satisfied with how I am showing up. I've been a verbal and physical leader. Also, I have been leading by vulnerability and example. It feels amazing to have confidence in myself to voice my opinions and to hold up boundaries, and not to worry about what others are thinking of me. I have so much more to tell you guys about my walkabout in the future.

I'll see you real soon! I love you both.

Carson

18.

Integrity = Being a man of your word

Graduation time! We arrive Sunday, February 16, in the evening. We are to meet Anne the next morning at basecamp so we can follow her up to Carson's latest location. We're excited to see him! Monday will be graduation, then we'll travel all day Tuesday to deliver him Wednesday to Balance House. We'll have him less than forty-eight hours. . . it's nerve-racking. What could go wrong? He won't jump out of a moving car . . . he won't leave in the middle of the night . . . he's changed, right?

We park on the forestry road and through the brush, I can see Carson hightailing it to us. He envelops me in a big hug! I love those hugs! He's excited to graduate. We have our last family session with Anne. We discuss expectations for the next thirty-six to forty-eight hours. Anne tells Carson to watch what he eats. His system has not had fats or sugars, especially processed, for three months. She says to be mindful of being in large crowds. It could be overwhelming. She encourages us to keep conversation light and to just catch up. Carson doesn't seem worried at all. Sloan and I are nervous wrecks, but are keeping it to ourselves.

The field staff lead us through the woods to this waterfall and cave-like structure. Along the way, the staff and some students create a path for Carson to walk, and as he goes from one section to another, they say wonderful things about him and give him words of encouragement. It feels like it could be a Native American coming-of-age process. It was quite intimate.

As we enter the cave, we circle around and again each person gives their impression of him with words of wisdom. All these kids have come so far. There are a few who just listen because they have only been in the group a short time. They are learning the process. I have always said that learning should be experiential and so much more is gained by the process than in the product. We wish them well.

It's time to say our goodbyes. Carson hugs all the staff and fellow students and then bear hugs Anne. He says he'll be back some day, but as field staff! We hug Anne and tell her we'll keep her updated. Carson jumps in the transport truck, and we follow behind. When we arrive back at base camp, Carson has to "debrief" and gets to take a shower. Forty-five minutes later, he appears all clean but still smelling of campfire smoke. They said that would linger on him for a good while. He is in the clothes we dropped him off in. They fit like they are supposed to. He gained about fifteen pounds in the woods. He was underweight when he went in. He says he's starved and wants to go for a burger and fries. "Well, so much for watching what you eat like

Anne said," I say as I roll my eyes. For the next thirty-six hours he eats and drinks everything in sight. It's amazing he isn't sick. He must have an iron gut.

Tuesday morning, we head out to catch a flight from Atlanta to Utah. He listens to his music and watches Netflix. He really doesn't want to talk a whole bunch. That's OK. We land in Utah, grab a bite, and head to our hotel. At 10:00 p.m., Carson decides he wants me to cut his hair for the second time in thirty-six hours. He makes me laugh. He hasn't lost his sense of fashion being in the wilderness.

Wednesday morning, we arrive at Balance House and are greeted by three really cool guys: Tony, Will, and Jon. I look at Sloan and whisper, "These guys will teach Carson that being sober is cool."

All three are in recovery. Will and Jon went through Balance House five or six years ago. They serve as the residents' case managers. Will is going to be Carson's. Tony explains the program and how it's imperative that the guys learn to make their own decisions. They'll have a better chance of staying sober when they are in control. He says that the guys are mentored, not managed. They believe in teaching what it means to be a man of your word. At that point he looks at Carson and says, "So, if you're not being a man of your word. I get to call bullshit. Got it?" Carson fully agrees! I really like these guys!

Will and Jon show us around the compound, and to Carson's part of the duplex. There are four duplexes and a main house. About twenty-seven guys ages eighteen to thirty live in Balance House. They need to check in and out of the main house every time they leave or come back. They are randomly drug tested and always breathalyzed. Communication is a key part to living at Balance House. We finish our tour and unload Carson's bags and say goodbye. Will says he'll call us in a couple days. He is taking Carson to get a cell phone and orient him. I didn't cry when we left him this time.

19.

I admitted I am powerless over my addiction, that my life had become unmanageable.

Step #1, 12step.org

Shortly after we return home from dropping Carson off at Balance House, COVID-19 enters the United States. The country shuts down. Everyone is to "shelter in place" till the scientists and government can figure out the next steps in keeping us all safe. It is by the grace of God we got Carson moved before the lockdown.

Carson starts his group therapy three times a week and by the end of the first week he is bored when not at group. He asks Will if he can get a job. Will agrees as long as it doesn't interfere with group. Will helps him to find a parks department job just down the street from Balance House. Carson is able to work all through Utah's shelter-in-place order, probably because he works outside.

Over the next several months, Carson sees his therapist, Melissa, at least once a week. Before the twelve-step programs shut down their in-person meetings, Carson was able to meet a guy a little older than him and asked him to be his sponsor. They have built a nice relationship, and Trevor is starting to encourage Carson to become a sponsor himself. He will once he has his year of sobriety under his belt. He is making good friends with the other guys at Balance House.

Carson continues to work and save money for a car and his hiking gear. He pays for his own food and phone, as well. He has come a long way from making money just to get high. He is learning to adult.

April 18, 2020, was his six-month sober birthday. He celebrated by taking an uber to the trailhead of Mt. Olympus and proceeded to hike and summit. At 9,000 feet he took a selfie to show his accomplishment. It took him five hours to ascend and two-and-a-half hours to descend. He called the next day. "Mom, my quads feel like that time when I caught for fourteen innings straight! The climb was so dope!"

20.

*Peace I leave with you; my peace I give
to you. I do not give to you as the world
gives. Do not let your hearts be troubled
and do not be afraid.*

John 14:27 (NIV)

In August 2020, we were able to visit Carson. It had been six months since we'd seen him last. He celebrated ten months sober shortly after we left. When we arrive, I call him from the driveway of Balance House. "Where are you?"

He says, "Where are you?!"

"We're in your driveway, by the office."

All I hear is silence. He's hung up. Immediately we see him running toward us. He swoops in to give me, the momma, a big ole bear hug! I can't help but tear up. I release my grip and look up to see he, too, has tears in his eyes. He looks so good.

"Carson, I think you've grown just since the wilderness. Let me check you against Dad." Sloan is 6'3", and Carson is just an inch shy of being head-to-head with him. His hair is

Coolio long and his skin is smooth and tan except for the beard growth.

A couple weeks before we arrived, he bought his first car with the money he saved from working these past six months. It's a black 2003 Jeep Grand Cherokee with a lift kit for all the off-roading he plans to do. I jump in his car and Sloan follows as we head to our Airbnb. He's able to stay with us for the week. In fact, while we are visiting, he is going to move to Phase 4, which is Beta. It's an apartment with a couple of roommates. He'll have more independence, which he's earned. He now will have to pay rent. We tell him we can pay the supplemental fee for another six months, then he'll have to go on his own.

While in Utah, we meet with Will, Jon, and Carson's therapist, Melissa. They all ask how we feel things are going and do we have any concerns? They feel he is doing great and meeting all the milestones. We agree.

I say, "Though as a momma, I have some worries . . . I think he smokes too much, and that he drinks too many Monsters. He doesn't sleep enough and he's not eating enough veg."

The guys, Will and Jon, just look at me with a bit of a smile and say, "Well, Dawn, we pick our battles around here. He's not using, and remember, he is nineteen."

Huh? Yep, that is true . . . I have to let go. I can't parent him from 1,300 miles away. He'll learn.

We ended up having a really nice family vacation, which hadn't happened in a long time. We hiked several peaks, rented a boat and wave runner for a day, and went for a lovely dinner in Park City. The "boys" still liked to roughhouse, even at twenty-one and nineteen. Sloan and I would halfheartedly say, "Well, we don't miss that." We had some good laughs just teasing each other.

The last day in Utah we sent Jackson and Maddie off to drive back to Indiana. Sloan, Carson, and I ran errands, had lunch, and then Carson and I went for mother-son tattoos. Sloan and Jackson didn't want to make it a family thing, but Carson had asked if I'd be willing to do that with him. How could I say no?

My tattoo says, "For them I'll risk it all." Carson's reads, "Because of her I will not fall."

Epilogue

Writing our story has been at times emotional, yet cathartic. There were times when I'd ask myself, "Should I be doing this? It will certainly be airing our dirty laundry." And, "Will it go anywhere?" Or even, "Will anyone read it?"

Then, I come across someone who is unaware of the drug epidemic that is plaguing our country, especially our youth. They get so surprised when I just give them a brief synopsis of what Carson and our family have been through. Because of these reactions, I continue on. God's little nudges.

Someone said I looked at peace in our photos from our visit with Carson. I feel peaceful, but it will be a long time before I am at peace. I know that addiction is a disease. I do as Carson does. I take it one day at a time.

Over the past three to four years, we have learned a lot. We have learned that the system is broken. Insurance does not cross state lines and quality recovery programs get lost in the weeds, so to speak. We were lucky to have family and friends help us do the research. Even Carson did his part. He found the wilderness programs that lead us to Blue Ridge. We would recommend hiring a therapeutic consultant. When you get to the level of care Carson needed, you need experts who have vetted these programs. I promise you there is a program that will fit your adolescent or young adult. These professionals can help. Another gift of advice is to go different. In addiction you must change people, places, and things. Don't be afraid. Our youth are resilient, they adapt, and they crave to be empowered, whether they know it or not. It takes ninety days to start cognitive change. Studies show if you can keep them in programming at least a year, percentages of staying sober go up.

Carson says that the addicted have to want to change to change. As parents, we say do whatever it takes to save your kid!

To continue the conversation on
adolescent addiction, please visit

www.adolescentaddictionandrecovery.com.

Adolescence

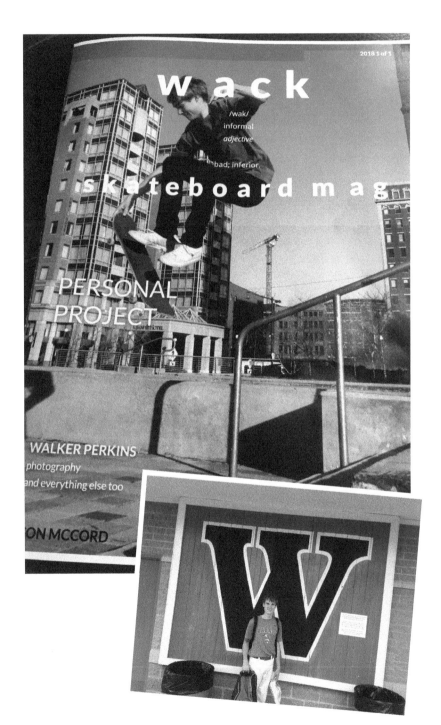

Addiction

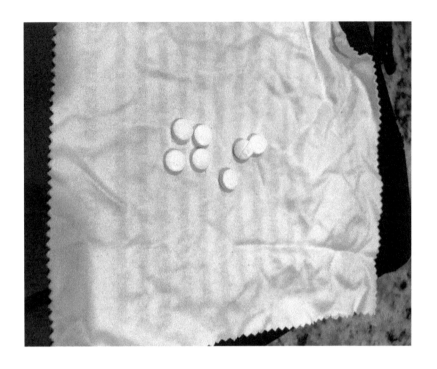

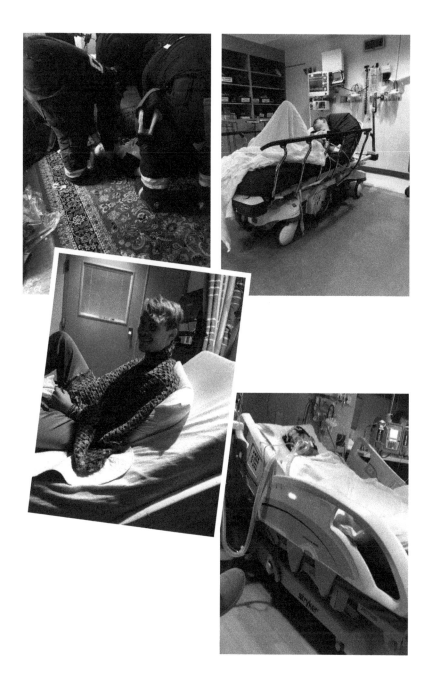

Recovery

Family visit

I've known Dawn McCord since her sons were toddlers and we met each other at church. She later became my hairdresser, which means that she also became my therapist in a way. During the conversations we have while she cuts my hair, we share experiences, opinions, our hopes and disappointments. Dawn has always greeted me with an aura of positivity, even during her darkest moments, and whatever clothes she may put on in the morning, she wears a cloak of faith at all times.

My heart broke with Dawn when she shared the stories of Carson's addiction, yet she always modeled strength and courage as well as authentic grief as she walked through the darkest valley a parent can know. As someone who loves people with substance abuse issues myself, I was inspired by her compassion, humility, and her ability to trust God with every step of the journey.

When Dawn told me that she was writing this book, I was once more in awe of her wisdom and generosity. The writing would be a healing mechanism for her, and at the same time she humbly offered up her own heartbreak as a gift of support and education for others.

When she asked me to paint the picture on the cover of this book, I was deeply honored. I can't remember when a commission has given me such a sense of purpose and responsibility. Creating the work became a walk in faith for me, and I felt God's presence as I set about expressing my experience of having witnessed the McCord Family's journey.

As an artist, I utilize symbolism in my work in various ways, and the image of Carson building a fire was no exception. Years earlier I was exploring one of my favorite shops, looking at stones, gems and various minerals. I discovered a beautifully colored stone called fuschite, a member of the mica family, with layers of pale green and a pearly luster. It was so intensely attractive to me that I purchased a couple small pieces to carry in my purse, and I looked up the metaphysical properties of the stone. Among other wonderful qualities, I read that it was meant to provide unconditional love and support for those in codependent relationships.

Imagine my delight when I discovered that one of my favorite brands of watercolors produced various jewel-toned paints that contained amounts of the actual mineral, ground down and used as pigment in the paint. Fuschite became one of my favorite "go-to " colors whenever I painted with watercolors. Considering the metaphysical properties of the stone, it only made sense that I used it generously in the painting of Carson, surrounding him with the gorgeous, sparkling gem tone the way we surround him with prayer.

Dawn's telling of the McCord Family's relationship with addiction is destined to offer love, support and education for people sharing this gut-wrenching journey, and it makes me feel incredibly grateful to be able to contribute in even a small way to the gift she is sharing with the world.

LorieLee Andrews

Acknowledgements

I'd like to thank David Sheff, author of *Beautiful Boy* and fellow parent of an addicted child, though your boy is a grown man now. Your book helped us to feel not so alone in navigating Carson's substance use. I spent many of nights reading sections of your book to my husband and crying. I'd say, "This is our life, too." You inspired me to write our story so that hopefully we can help another family not feel so alone.

I'd like to thank LorieLee Andrews for her beautiful artwork of our boy. Your talent amazes me. I am grateful to you for encouraging me to continue writing and to publish. Thanks to Jack, LorieLee's son. I so appreciate your patience in creating the cover!

Our thankfulness extends to Allison, Sarah, Matt, Stephanie, Cathy, and all the AGSes at Fairbanks in Indianapolis, Indiana. You all are amazing! Thank you for never giving up on him!

To Anne at Blue Ridge Therapeutic Wilderness, you saved our boy and taught us that "different" is the way to go. You taught me to express my feelings as opposed to the teaching/parenting mode I had pigeonholed myself in. I look forward to Carson coming back to BRTW to be your field staff!

A huge thank you goes to those field staff at BRTW who live with the kids in the wilderness at a minimum of six days a stretch. Ya'll Rock! My boy's hygiene hasn't been the same since the wilderness.

Thank you, thank you, thank you to Kim at One Oak Consulting! You are a Godsend!

To the guys Tony, Will, Jon, Mason, and Megan (I think the residents think you're a guy,) at Balance House, thank you for mentoring my boy and keeping him to "being a man of his word." He has learned and continues to learn a lot about adulting. Thanks to ya'll, sober is cool! Will, I am starting to lose my "twitch," but I think it's because I'm not getting a text from you saying "hey, can you talk?"

Huge thanks goes to Melissa at The Bloc! We appreciate your support of our family but most importantly you are my son's confidant!

To all our family: Brownells, Mauses, McCords, Shepherds, Stracks... Carson wouldn't be where he is if it weren't for all of your generous and loving support. Sloan, Carson, and I are so humbly grateful.

To all our friends: Merns and husbands, Church Chix and Dix, Church friends, Book Club, Funatics, OG-GNO and hubbies, Michelle G., Short Ridge/CFI friends, and our TT, your mercy and grace, love and support have shown us that friends are family too!

To Mr. O'Day and Mr. Pactor—talk about Grace with a capital G! Thank you for not giving up on Carson and for allowing him to finish high school before leaving the state.

To all our pastors: Rob and Susan, Carolyn and Andrew, Dave and Jamalyn, Kevin, Mindie, Heather, and our Big Guy Josh. You all were there, whether distracting him, babysitting him in Haiti, checking in with us, praying over him at his hospital bed—the list goes on. We are so grateful to have such a supportive church family!

Please know that the street goes both ways. We love each and every one of you and would be your support in a heartbeat.

To over a hundred people—friends, family, clients, and strangers—who donated to the Plumfund, words cannot express the gratitude we feel. It was your generosity that gave us hope that we could send Carson out of state.

To my husband, Sloan, my oldest son, Jackson, and Jackson's girlfriend, Maddie, we have been in the trenches together. I appreciate you all and thank you for letting me share our story. I love you!

To my baby boy, Carson, I will always support your recovery! Thank you for your transparency in sharing your story. We can only hope and pray that it will help other families. I love you!

Most importantly, I would like to recognize all the parents like Kelly, Joey's mom, and other parents who have lost a child to addiction. This disease is brutal. It produces gaping holes in the soul. This book is dedicated to you.

Carson's Afterword

My name is Carson. I am the person this book centers around. Currently it is October 8, 2020, ten days short from it being one year since my heroin overdose. If you ask me, this year has gone by pretty damn fast. Since I have arrived here in Utah, I've accomplished so many things I never thought I would at such a young age. I'm nineteen. I live in an apartment that I pay rent for. I buy my own groceries. I fully purchased my car on my own. You might be thinking, "Well these are pretty normal things for a kid your age." In one sense, you are right, but, I, Carson Sloan McCord, have a disease. Not only am I aware of this, but I have learned to embrace it. I have to. There is no hiding from my demons. They are persistent and lethal and their grasp is strong.

Being a teen in recovery is not easy. In fact, it's scary in a lot of ways. Ever since my freshman year of high school, I have been in and out of rehab. I constantly think, What's wrong with me? Why am I so different? What will the people at school think? What will their parents think? I'm a bad kid. As you can tell, my fear of judgement weighs heavily on me. I have never liked to disappoint people. I have always needed people around me to think everything was fine, that I wasn't struggling, and that I had it all under control. I like to have control, and if I don't have it, then I do everything possible to make myself think I do. There's a lot of comfort in having control. With that being said, I would always put on a mask, a front, an alternate, fake personality. This mask had a big smile on it that portrayed a perfect, happy life. I got really good at wearing this mask. I even wore it at my lowest. This was a huge manipulation and lie to the people around me. The less people who knew I had a problem in the first place, the more people I could fool and the more I could use without carrying around a guilty conscience. I thought I was blending in. In the end, it pulled me away from my loved ones.

I see now that as an addict, my number one priority was to get high and stay high. As time went on and my addiction progressed, I gradually stopped hanging out with my childhood best friends. I surrounded myself with new people whom I had met through experimenting with my newfound love of hard drugs. The last thing you want to hear when snorting a line of heroin or coke or popping a Xanax is, "Carson, you need help." Or "You shouldn't be doing that." Let me tell you, you will not hear that from someone who is making the exact same decisions as you. It's just easier that way.

Lately, I have been feeling very lonely in recovery. Being nineteen, I find that most of the friends I have made in the past year don't have plans to stay sober long term like I do. A lot of them are only doing it because their families sent them to a program. Once the program is finished, they will go back to doing what they were doing before, drinking and drugging. It's hard for me because I am in this for the long run. I get to know these guys really well and build strong relationships. As their recovery train runs out for them, I lose yet another close friend to drugs and alcohol. I don't blame them for this, because I am aware that most people my age haven't hit the rock bottom that I was at, and they haven't seen their life become so unmanageable. It's not easy for someone who is nineteen to want to be sober and live in recovery when they haven't yet been to Hell and back. I have a feeling this is how my friends back home felt as they watched me fall down the rabbit hole. It's ironic how everything comes back around one way or another.

Today is October 18, 2020. As much as I would love to say that I am celebrating one year sober, I cannot. On September 15, 2020, I made a choice to drink a few beers with my roommate. The day after I had instant regret and shame regarding my actions. How could I just throw away nearly a year of sobriety out the window, so easily?! The guilt and shame I was carrying brought me to tears. I immediately reached out for help from my supports whom I had acquired over the past eleven months. Of course, as always, the first person I called was my momma. Long story short, I'm working with my sponsor and he is taking me through the steps again. This is not to disregard all the hard work I have done in the past year. All the knowledge I attained is still there. Although, now, October 18 isn't my sobriety birthday anymore, it still and always will be a day to be celebrated by my family and me. This day is the day God gave me a second chance at life.

Overall, for me, it's about living in the process. I can't think about the end goal (being sober for the rest of my life), because then I get overwhelmed and it seems impossible. I just tell myself, "Okay, I'm going to be sober for today." Then before I know it, hopefully, I'll have twenty years under my belt. Obviously, it's not that easy. Just because I make a conscience decision to be sober, doesn't mean life around me is "sober." Life can bring pretty terrible things across your path. That is what I am preparing for right now. Although my life is going really well at the moment, I understand that it won't always be that way. I have to learn how to cope and stay sober through the toughest parts of life. I realize that a big part of being successful in sobriety is to give back and to serve others, like so many have done for me along my journey.

I am so thankful God has given me this chance to continue my journey. Sober.

Resources

Bradley, Michael J. *Yes, Your Teen is Crazy! Loving Your Kid without Losing Your Mind.* Harbor Press, 2003.

Foote, Jeffrey, Wilkens, Carrie, Kosanke, Nicole, and Higgs, Stephanie. *Beyond Addiction: How Science and Kindness Help People Change.* Scribner, 2014.

Jensen, Frances E., and Nutt, Amy Ellis. *The Teenage Brain: A Neuroscientist's Survival Guide to Raising Adolescents and Young Adults.* Harper Collins, 2015.

Kindlon, Dan, and Thompson, Michael. *Raising Cain: Protecting the Emotional Life of Boys.* Ballantine Books, 1999; Random House, 2000.

Pozatek, Krissy. *The Parallel Process: Growing Alongside Your Adolescent or Young Adult Child in Treatment.* Lantern Books, 2010.

The Parent's 20 Minute Guide: A Guide for Parents about How to Help Their Children Change Their Substance Use (2nd ed.). CMC: Center for Motivation & Change, 2016.

Ramesh, Divya, Schlosburg, Joel E., and Lichtman, Aron H., Weibelhaus, Jason "Marijuana Dependence: Not Just Smoke and Mirrors." *ILAR journal/National Research Council, Institute of Laboratory Animal January 2011* https://www.researchgate.net/publication/235402080_Marijuana_Dependence_Not_Just_Smoke_and_Mirrors

Schaeffer, Dick. *Choices & Consequences: What to do When a Teenager Uses Alcohol/Drugs.* Hazelden Publishing, 1987, pp. 27, 28, 30.

Sheff, David. *Beautiful Boy: A Father's Journey through His Son's Addiction.* Houghton Mifflin Harcourt, 2008, p. 312.

Swendsen, Joel, Burstein, Marcy, and Meikangas, Kathleen R. "Use and Abuse of Alcohol and Illicit Drugs in US Adolescents: Results of the National Comorbidity Survey-Adolescent Supplement." *Archives of General Psychiatry,* 2012 https://www.ncbi.nlm.nih.gov/pmc/articles/PMC3746542/

TIME (Special Edition). *The Science of Addiction.* 2019/2020.

Blue Ridge Therapeutic Wilderness
(888) 914-1050
Admissions@BlueRidgeWilderness.com
236 File Street
Clayton, GA 30525

Center for Motivation & Change
www.motivationandchange.com
276 Fifth Avenue Suite 1101
New York, NY 10001

Fairbanks (Community) Recovery Center
(800) 225-4673
www.Fairbankscd.org
8102 Clearvista Parkway
Indianapolis, IN 46256

National Institute on Drug Abuse
www.drugabuse.gov

One Oak Therapeutic Consulting
(773) 661-8182
www.OneOakConsult.com

Partnership to End Addiction
www.drugfree.org

Shatterproof
info@shatterproof.org
101 Merritt 7 Corporate Park, 1st floor
Norwalk, CT 06851

The Substance Abuse and Mental Health Services
Administration
www.samhsa.gov

Twelve-Step Programs:

www.al-anon.org

www.aa.org

www.na.org

www.ca.org

Thanks to J. Cole. Lyrics from his "Motiv8" (KOD, Dreamville Records, Roc Nation, Interscope Records, 2018) used by permission.

CPSIA information can be obtained
at www.ICGtesting.com
Printed in the USA
LVHW072031080122
708111LV00028B/254